Praxis Guide

for

Slavin

Educational Psychology
Theory and Practice

Ninth Edition

prepared by

Janet Medina
McDaniel College

PEARSON

Boston   New York   San Francisco
Mexico City   Montreal   Toronto   London   Madrid   Munich   Paris
Hong Kong   Singapore   Tokyo   Cape Town   Sydney

ISBN-13: 978-0-205-62639-7
ISBN-10:   0-205-62639-4

Printed in the United States of America

10 9 8 7 6 5 4 3 2 1   12 11 10 09 08

Contents

SECTION 1: GENERAL PRAXIS TEST INFORMATION

Description of *The Praxis Series*®

The Praxis Series® is comprised of three separate tests: the Praxis I, II, and III. The Praxis I test is also referred to as the PPST or Pre-Professional Skills Test. According to *The Praxis Series*® homepage on the ETS Web site (www.ets.org/praxis/), these three tests are intended to mark three major milestones of teacher development: 1) entering a teacher-training program, 2) licensure for entering the teaching profession, and 3) the first year of teaching. Currently, thirty-five states require prospective teachers to pass at least one of the Praxis tests. Other states and professional organizations (e.g., National Association of School Psychologists) also use the Praxis tests in some form. Information on qualification standards by state and organization is available at: www.ets.org/praxis/prxstate.html. Some states (e.g., New York) use their own teacher certification exams.

The formats for Praxis I and Praxis II tests include scenarios, case histories, and comprehensive reading. Conceptual knowledge, procedural knowledge, and representations of quantitative information are assessed on the Praxis I, and organizing content knowledge, creating an environment for student learning, and teacher professionalism are assessed on the Praxis II. You can download the national Praxis Series Registration Bulletin at: www.ets.org/praxis/prxreg.html. The bulletin provides information necessary to apply for the Praxis I and Praxis II tests. There is a separate registration bulletin for those taking the Praxis II in California, accessible at the same site. The above website also provides individual links to test centers and dates, as well as other registration options.

<u>Examinees Whose Primary Language is Not English (PLNE)</u>

Nonstandard test administrations (extended testing time) may be available for test takers whose primary language is not English. Test takers who meet ETS requirements will be allowed 50 percent additional testing time. ETS requires test takers whose primary language is not English to provide documentation to support the request for extended test time. Detailed information including specific guidelines for documentation, available accommodations, contact information, etc. may be accessed in the Praxis registration bulletin, p. 9: http://ets.org/Media/Tests/PRAXIS/pdf/01361.pdf. Relevant forms may be found on p. 18 and p. 19.

<u>Test Takers With Disabilities</u>

The Praxis Series program administered by ETS is committed to serving test takers with disabilities by providing assistance and reasonable accommodations appropriate to the purpose of each test. Nonstandard testing accommodations are available for test takers who meet ETS requirements. Depending upon the specific needs of the individual, accommodations may include, but are not limited to: extended test time, test reader, scribe, sign language interpreter (for directions only), access to specific assistive technology (e.g., Kensington Trackball Mouse, Intellikeys keyboard, etc.), and alternate test formats (e.g., enlarged print, audio recording, and

Braille). Individuals must provide sufficient documentation to support the request for test accommodations, and, in some cases, ETS may need up to six weeks to process the request. Recency of documentation may need to be anywhere from 6 months to 5 years, depending on the disability in question. Effective July 1, 2004, accommodations approved for test takers with disabilities for extended testing time will be provided on a section-by-section basis. For example, depending on the nature of the disability, a test taker may be approved for extended time on the quantitative section of the PRAXIS I but receive standard time on the reading section. Plan carefully. Detailed information, including specific guidelines for documentation, available accommodations, contact information, etc. may be accessed at the following website: http://www.ets.org/praxis/prxdsabl.html.

Praxis I/PPST

The PPST assesses basic competencies in reading, mathematics, and writing. The intent is to give students the opportunity to assess basic skills before spending time, money, and energy training to become teachers. For state-by-state passing scores on the Praxis I test, see www.ets.org/praxis/prxstate.html. Some states allow for individualized passing test scores and/or cumulative test scores, which then allows a test taker to pass Praxis I by electing to use the sum of all three test scores – this is especially helpful if the examinee has clear strengths or weaknesses in a particular area. For example, Maryland requires examinees to obtain scores of at least 177 in Reading, 173 in Writing, and 177 in Mathematics or a composite score of 527. Applicants may meet the testing requirement by submitting either individual passing scores or a composite score that is at or above the state qualifying score. Therefore, as a sample, if a test taker obtains a score of 175 in Reading and 170 in Writing, as long as the individual obtains a score of at least 182 in Mathematics, for a cumulative score of 527, the test taker will pass Praxis I.

The Praxis I test can be taken in a traditional paper-based format at many colleges and universities throughout the U.S. and U.S. Territories, as well as select locations outside of the U.S., about four times a year. It is important to note that the PPST is not offered at every test center on every date. The Reading and Mathematics paper-based tests each consist of 40 multiple-choice questions and each are given over a 60 minute time period. The Writing paper-based test consists of 38 multiple-choice questions given over a 30 minute time period, as well as one writing essay given in a 30 minute time period. ETS does not place any limits on the number of times a test taker may retake a paper-based test, though some states and colleges or universities may place their own restrictions.

The Praxis I can also be taken as a computer-based test (CBT). The CBT format is tailored to each candidate's performance, and provides different question types and immediate scoring. Your Reading and Mathematics scores will appear on the computer as soon as you complete your tests. Because all essays are sent to ETS for scoring, your Writing test score will not be available immediately. Within two to three weeks, ETS will mail an official score report for all tests to you and to your designated score recipients. Computer-based tests are offered as single tests and take two hours per test, allowing time for tutorials and collection of personal information. The Computerized PPST in Reading, Mathematics, and Writing is also offered as a combined test that is delivered as a single testing session over 4 ½ hours. If your keyboarding or word processing skills are limited, this option is not recommended. The Reading and Mathematics tests each consist of 46 questions over a 75 minute time period; the Writing test consists of 44 questions over a 38 minute time period, as well as one essay in a 30 minute time period. Computer-based testing is available at Prometric^{TM} Testing Centers (many Prometric Testing Centers are located inside Sylvan Learning Centers), as well as some colleges and universities and ETS Field Offices, throughout the U.S., across U.S. Territories, in Puerto Rico, and at sites in Canada. If you want to take the CBT, you can call 1-800-853-6773 for a Prometric^{TM} test site near you. In addition, ETS maintains a current list of CBT test sites on their website at: http://etsis4.ets.org/tcenter/cbt_dm.cfm. Individuals who are Deaf or Hard of Hearing and use a TTY should call the following number instead: 1-800-529-3590 or for ETS Customer Service, you may call: 609-771-7714. All test takers may only take the CBT once within a calendar month and no more frequently then six times within a 12-month period. More information about CBT is available at the following site: www.ets.org/praxis/prxcbt.html.

The fee for the Praxis I test varies depending on the format and how many tests are taken at once. The paper-based test requires a one-time registration fee of $50 that is applicable for one calendar year. For more information on both versions of the Praxis I test visit the following site: www.ets.org/praxis/prxpIoption.html.

The following chart contains the basic data about the Praxis I Paper-based tests.

Code	Test	Time	No. of Questions	Format	Content	Score Range
10710	PPST Reading	60 mins.	40	Multiple Choice	1. Literal comprehension 2. Critical and inferential comprehension	150-190
10730	PPST Math [Calculators are prohibited]	60 mins.	40	Multiple Choice	1. Conceptual knowledge 2. Procedural knowledge 3. Quantitative information 4. Geometry 5. Formal mathematical reasoning	150-190
20720	PPST Writing	30 mins.	45	Multiple Choice	Use of English grammar	150-190
		30 mins.		Essay	Requires writing an essay on an assigned topic.	

The following chart contains the basic data about the Praxis I Computer-based (CBT) tests.

Code	Test	Time	No. of Questions	Format	Content	Score range
5710	PPST Reading	60 min.	40	Multiple-choice questions based on reading passages and statement	I. Literal comprehension II. Critical and inferential comprehension	150 -190
5730	PPST Math [Calculators are prohibited]	75 min.	46	Multiple-choice questions	I. Conceptual knowledge and procedural knowledge II. Representations of quantitative information III. Measurement and informal geometry; formal mathematical reasoning	150 -190
5720	PPST Writing	68 min. (38 min. MC & 30 min. essay)	44 / 1	Multiple-choice questions / Essay	I. Grammatical relationships II. Structural relationships III. Idiom/Word choice, mechanics, and no error IV. Essay	150 -190

Praxis II

The Praxis II tests consist of over 120 Subject Assessments/Speciality Area tests for teachers, general tests covering Principles of Learning and Teaching (PLT tests), and Teaching Foundations Tests. The Subject Assessments, administered in multiple-choice and constructed response test format, measure general and subject-related teaching knowledge and skills. The Teaching Foundations Tests focus on pedagogy in multi-subject (elementary), English, Language Arts, Mathematics, Science and Social Science through multiple-choice and constructed response formats. The Principles of Learning and Teaching (PLT) tests – 30521 [Early Childhood], 30522 [Grades K-6], 30523 [Grades 5-9], and 30524 [Grades 7-12] – measure general pedagogical knowledge at four grade levels, using case studies, multiple-choice, and constructed response formats, and are where you will encounter questions concerning educational psychology. Therefore, they are the primary focus of this Praxis guide. According to the ETS, the content tests are regularly updated, and several are available in each subject field. As a result, a state can customize its program by selecting those assessments that best match its own licensure requirements. The ETS website www.ets.org/praxis/prxtest.html provides more information on the structure of the 140 content tests. The ETS website www.ets.org/praxis/prxstate.html provides specific state requirements for content tests. Because many states norm-reference Praxis scores, passing scores are likely to change often. So, be sure to keep yourself up to date of all necessary information by checking the above website periodically.

The following chart contains basic data about the Praxis II: Principles of Learning and Teaching.

Test Code	Test Name	Time	Number of questions	Format	Topics covered
30521	Principles of Learning and Teaching Early Childhood	2 hours	12 short-answer question and 24 multiple-choice questions	4 case histories, each followed by 3 short-answer question; 24 multiple-choice questions, in two 12-question sections	I. Students as Learners (multiple-choice questions) - 11% II. Instruction and Assessment (multiple-choice questions) - 11% III. Teacher Professionalism (multiple-choice questions) - 11% IV. Students as Learners (short-answer questions) - 22% V. Instruction and Assessment (short-answer questions) - 22% VI. Communication Techniques (short-answer questions) - 11% VII. Teacher Professionalism (short-answer questions) - 11%
30522	Principles of Learning and Teaching Grades K-6	2 hours	12 short-answer question and 24 multiple-choice questions	4 case histories, each followed by 3 short-answer question; 24 multiple-choice questions, in two 12-question sections	I. Students as Learners (multiple-choice questions) - 11% II. Instruction and Assessment (multiple-choice questions) - 11% III. Teacher Professionalism (multiple-choice questions) - 11% IV. Students as Learners (short-answer questions) - 22% V. Instruction and Assessment (short-answer questions) - 22% VI. Communication Techniques (short-answer questions) - 11% VII. Teacher Professionalism (short-answer questions) - 11%
30523	Principles of Learning and Teaching Grades 5-9	2 hours	12 short-answer question and 24 multiple-choice questions	4 case histories, each followed by 3 short-answer question; 24 multiple-choice questions, in two 12-question sections	I. Students as Learners (multiple-choice questions) - 11% II. Instruction and Assessment (multiple-choice questions) - 11% III. Teacher Professionalism (multiple-choice questions) - 11% IV. Students as Learners (short-answer questions) - 22% V. Instruction and Assessment (short-answer questions) - 22% VI. Communication Techniques (short-answer questions) - 11% VII. Teacher Professionalism (short-answer questions) - 11%
30524	Principles of Learning and Teaching Grades 7-12	2 hours	12 short-answer question and 24 multiple-choice questions	4 case histories, each followed by 3 short-answer question; 24 multiple-choice questions, in two 12-question sections	I. Students as Learners (multiple-choice questions) - 11% II. Instruction and Assessment (multiple-choice questions) - 11% III. Teacher Professionalism (multiple-choice questions) - 11% IV. Students as Learners (short-answer questions) - 22% V. Instruction and Assessment (short-answer questions) - 22% VI. Communication Techniques (short-answer questions) - 11% VII. Teacher Professionalism (short-answer questions) - 11%

The following chart contains basic data about the Praxis II: Teaching Foundations Tests

Test Code	Test Name	Time	Number of questions	Format	Content categories
10088	Teaching Foundations: Social Science	4 hours	52	Multiple-choice questions (50) and constructed response (2)	I. Human Development – 5-6% II. Addressing Learning Differences and Special Needs – 5–6% III. Working with English Learners - 5–6% IV. Reading Instruction - 5–6% V. Assessment of Student Progress - 5–6% VI. Classroom Management Techniques - 5–6% VII. Teaching Methods in Social Science, Middle/Junior High Level - 32–33% VIII. Teaching Methods in Social Science, High School Level - 32–33%
10068	Teaching Foundations: Mathematics	4 hours	52	Multiple-choice questions (50) and constructed response (2)	I. Human Development – 5-6% II. Addressing Learning Differences and Special Needs – 5–6% III. Working with English Learners - 5–6% IV. Reading Instruction - 5–6% V. Assessment of Student Progress - 5–6% VI. Classroom Management Techniques - 5–6% VII. Teaching Methods in Mathematics, Middle/Junior High Level - 32–33% VIII. Teaching Methods in Mathematics, High School Level - 32–33%
10048	Teaching Foundations: English	4 hours	52	Multiple-choice questions (50) and constructed response (2)	I. Human Development – 5-6% II. Addressing Learning Differences and Special Needs – 5–6% III. Working with English Learners - 5–6% IV. Reading Instruction - 5–6% V. Assessment of Student Progress - 5–6% VI. Classroom Management Techniques - 5–6% VII. Teaching Methods in English, Middle/Junior High Level - 32–33% VIII. Teaching Methods in English, High School Level - 32–33%
10438	Teaching Foundations: Science	4 hours	52	Multiple-choice questions (50) and constructed response (2)	I. Human Development – 5-6% II. Addressing Learning Differences and Special Needs – 5–6% III. Working with English Learners - 5–6% IV. Reading Instruction - 5–6% V. Assessment of Student Progress - 5–6% VI. Classroom Management Techniques - 5–6% VII. Teaching Methods in Science, Middle/Junior High Level - 32–33% VIII. Teaching Methods in Science, High School Level - 32–33%

| 10528 | Teaching Foundations: Multiple Subjects | 4 hours | 52 | Multiple-choice questions (50) and constructed response (4) | I. Human Development – 6-7%
II. Learning Differences and Special Needs; Helping English Learners – 13-14%
III. Assessment of Student Progress - 6–7%
IV. Classroom Management Techniques - 6–7%
V. Teaching Methods in English - 16–17%
VI. Teaching Methods in Social Science - 16–17%
V. Teaching Methods in Mathematics - 16–17%
V. Teaching Methods in Science - 16–17% |

The following chart contains the Praxis II Subject Assessments and codes.

Content Tests

10700	Agriculture
10900	Agriculture (PA)
10780	Agriculture (CA)
10133	Art: Content Knowledge
20132	Art: Content, Traditions, Criticism and Aesthetics
20131	Art Making
10340	Audiology
20030	Biology and General Science
30233	Biology: Content Essays
20231	Biology Content Knowledge, Part I
20232	Biology: Content Knowledge, Part II
20235	Biology: Content Knowledge
10100	Business Education
30242	Chemistry: Content Essays
20241	Chemistry: Content Knowledge
20245	Chemistry: Content Knowledge
10070	Chemistry: Physics and General Science
10087	Citizenship Education: Content Knowledge
20800	Communication (PA)
10810	Cooperative Education
10867	Driver Education
10022	Early Childhood: Content Knowledge
10020	Early Childhood Education
20571	Earth and Space Sciences: Content Knowledge
10910	Economics
10271	Education of Deaf and Hard of Hearing Students
20353	Education of Exceptional Students: Core and Content Knowledge
10382	Education of Exceptional Students: Learning Disabilities
10542	Education of Exceptional Students: Mild to Moderate Disabilities
10544	Education of Exceptional Students: Severe to Profound Disabilities
20021	Education of Young Children
10410	Educational Leadership: Administration and Supervision

20012	Elementary Education.: Content Area Exercises
10014	Elementary Education: Content Knowledge
10011	Elementary Education.: Curriculum, Instruction, and Assessment
10016	Elementary Education: Curriculum, Instruction, and Assessment K - 5
10041	English Language, Literature, and Composition: Content Knowledge
20042	English Language, Literature, and Composition: Essays
30043	English Language, Literature, and Composition: Pedagogy
20360	English to Speakers of Other Languages
10830	Environmental Education
10120	Family and Consumer Sciences
10840	Foreign Language Pedagogy
20173	French: Content Knowledge
10173	French: Content Knowledge
10171	French: Productive Language Skills
30511	Fundamental Subjects: Content Knowledge
30067	General Mathematics (WV)
30433	General Science: Content Essays
10431	General Science: Content Knowledge Part 1
10432	General Science: Content Knowledge Part 2
10435	General Science: Content Knowledge
30920	Geography
20181	German: Content Knowledge
30182	German: Productive Language Skills
10357	Gifted Education
10930	Government/Political Science
20856	Health and Physical Education: Content Knowledge
20550	Health Education
10200	Introduction to the Teaching of Reading
10600	Latin
10310	Library Media Specialist
30234	Life Science: Pedagogy
10560	Marketing Education
10061	Mathematics: Content Knowledge
30065	Mathematics: Pedagogy
20063	Mathematics: Proofs, Models, and Problems Part 1

20146	Middle School: Content Knowledge
10049	Middle School English Language Arts
20069	Middle School Mathematics
10439	Middle School Science
20089	Middle School Social Studies
20112	Music: Analysis
30111	Music: Concepts and Processes
10113	Music: Content Knowledge
10091	Physical Education : Content Knowledge
30092	Physical Education: Movement Forms-Analysis and Design
20093	Physical Education: Movement Forms-Video Evaluation
20481	Physical Science: Content Knowledge
30483	Physical Science-Pedagogy
30262	Physics: Content Essays
10261	Physics: Content Knowledge
10265	Physics: Content Knowledge
20530	Pre-Kindergarten Education
20390	Psychology
20201	Reading Across the Curriculum: Elementary
20202	Reading Across the Curriculum: Secondary
20300	Reading Specialist
10860	Safety/Driver Education
20420	School Guidance and Counseling
10400	School Psychologist
20211	School Social Worker: Content Knowledge
10951	Social Sciences: Content Knowledge
20082	Social Studies: Analytical Essays
10081	Social Studies: Content Knowledge
20085	Social Studies: Interpretation and Analysis
20083	Social Studies: Interpretation of Materials
30084	Social Studies: Pedagogy
20950	Sociology
10191	Spanish: Content Knowledge
30194	Spanish: Pedagogy
20192	Spanish: Productive Language Skills

10352	Special Education: Application of Core Principles Across Categories of Disability
20351	Special Education: Knowledge-based Core Principles
10690	Special Education: Preschool/Early Childhood
20371	Special Education: Teaching Students with Behavioral Disorders/Emotional Disturbances
20381	Special Education: Teaching Students with Learning Disabilities
20321	Special Education: Teaching Students with Mental Retardation
10220	Speech Communication
20330	Speech-Language Pathology
10880	Teaching Speech to Students with Language Impairments
10290	Teaching Students with Orthopedic Impairments
10280	Teaching Students with Visual Impairments
10050	Technology Education
10640	Theatre
10890	Vocational General Knowledge
10940	World and US History
10941	World and US History: Content Knowledge

Praxis III: Classroom Performance Assessments

The Praxis III test usually takes place during a teacher's first year of service. According to *The Praxis Series® Tests at a Glance* booklet:

> *Praxis 3 classroom performance assessments are used at the beginning teaching level to evaluate all aspects of a beginning teacher's classroom performance. Designed to assist in making licensure decisions, these comprehensive assessments are conducted in the classroom by trained local assessors who employ a set of nationally validated criteria. (p. 5)*

I) Test-Taking Tips

The following are test-taking tips compiled from a variety of sources, including the ETS Praxis guides, students who have taken the Praxis tests, and the combined experience of colleagues myself teaching numerous courses at the post-secondary level. However, I begin with a brief discussion on how your approach to learning may influence your test results.

General Philosophical Approach to Test-Taking

Clearly, your goal is to pass the Praxis test the first time. Nobody wishes to repeat a test several times; it is inconvenient and costly. As such, the goal of this guide is to help prepare you to pass the Praxis the first and only time you take it. However, there are no guarantees. One way to increase your odds of passing the Praxis test, though, is to develop an adaptive approach to learning. Although you have been in school for many years now, and undoubtedly are keen learners, there is always room for improvement. If you were not interested in improving your study skills, you would not be wasting time reading this text. What follows then is a brief description of mastery learning as it applies to postsecondary students, followed by test-taking tips for the period before taking the Praxis test, and tips for the day of the test.

Basic Learning Skills

Learning is a process, not an end. The aim is to master content, not memorize facts. If you focus on mastering content, you will be far better prepared for any test than if you focus merely on memorizing facts. Besides, facts will not help you become a better teacher. Even if you teach a course like History that relies on knowledge of facts, the best learners memorize the facts because of their extreme interest in the topic, not by rote. Interest results in awareness of content deficiencies. This awareness motivates the good learner to look deeper into the topic until the learner is so absorbed in the material that memorization is no longer the goal, but the inevitable outcome of the process. So, immerse yourself into your preparation, not because you just want to pass the test, but because you want to be an excellent teacher.

The learning process is a road filled with obstacles, and where there are obstacles, you are bound to take a couple of errant steps. Errors are a part of learning. Think of errors as your allies, not your enemies; they provide feedback that aims future efforts on target. If you are a good learner, you will take this feedback and double your efforts to understand the content you are lacking.

If you think you know everything, you are fooling yourself. It is a fallacy to believe you know all there is to know. You may graduate from the program with the best reputation for producing good teachers, but you still are a relative infant next to an experienced teacher. Experienced teachers have learned to balance their knowledge with the ambiguity of classroom reality. Every day they experience circumstances that no teaching program can anticipate completely. This is key, because the officials producing educational tests like the Praxis, and those depending on their results, are keenly interested in seeing how well you react to unforeseen circumstances. Thus, if you prepare yourself to pass the Praxis by memorizing facts, without a deeper understanding of the teaching and learning process, and variability in the students you will teach, you will trip easily on ambiguity. To improve your chances of solving ambiguous items, and dealing with unforeseen circumstances as a teacher, enter each situation with a deep understanding of the fundamental principles underlying key teaching issues. My favorite way to increase depth of conceptual understanding is to have students mentally "play" with concepts learned in text, applying them to their daily lives. For instance, issues like dealing with disruptive students are highly debatable, as there are many approaches to the student discipline. Take time, observe your surroundings and watch how others deal with disruptive children and adolescents, in class and in the non-school environment. Ask yourself the following questions: what is the situation? What are the circumstances surrounding the situation? What would I do in this situation? What would be the consequences of my actions? By mentally playing with concepts, you will have a deeper understanding of concepts, and you will anticipate many problems you will face on exams and in the classroom. This should improve your chances of passing all tests you take in the future, paper and pencil or real.

The take home message to these suggestions is that learning is a never-ending process that requires continued self-observation, and much effort.

Before the Test

- Complete many practice tests. Comfort and familiarity with the test format are learned skills. (ETS)

- Work on essay writing skills. You must be able to incorporate the pedagogical content in your essay.

- Study with a friend. You can learn from your peers. Take turns teaching each other concepts. Teaching is an excellent way to learn concepts!

- Create vocabulary drill cards. Start by referring to the chapter reviews and glossary in your textbook. Have a friend drill you on the vocabulary found there. Have your friend mark the terms you don't know. You can create your vocabulary drill cards from those words. Use an 81/2 x 11 sheet folded in half. Put the terms on the left side and the definitions on the right. Writing the information on a drill card will also help you remember the facts. This process will help you with the case studies and provide you with content for your essays.

- Vocabulary notecards are another way to enhance your knowledge of terminology and other important information. Use 3 X 5 or 5 X 7 index cards. On one side of the card write the term or phrase or other important information (such as an important federal law number or name, like IDEA). On the other side write an accurate definition in your own words and then use the term, phrase, or other information in a sentence. This gives you a chance to study by yourself or with a friend, and also an opportunity to try to make the information relevant to you, rather than just simply using rote memorization.

- Be prepared to write responses to classroom scenarios. Readers do not want lengthy answers, so learn to condense information. Be succinct! One way to do this is to write and trim your responses. What is the best way to get your message across with the least amount of words?

- Revisit basic mathematics and geography facts for the Elementary Content/Specialty tests.

- Do not plan to leave as soon as you finish the test. You have to stay the entire time. You also will probably need the entire time provided for the essay portion. This means you have time to review your responses, and make changes where necessary. Therefore, when practicing test questions, also try to time yourself and practice budgeting your time so that you won't find yourself rushing to finish the last questions during the actual test.

- Know how to deal with children's behaviors in the classroom. One essay question asked about handling "copying" in the classroom.

- Go to bed early. This is a serious test. You will have much time for enjoyment and relaxation after the test is completed.

The Day of the Test

- Tests start at the exact time; do not be late!

- You must bring a picture ID to the testing center. (ETS)

- Bring three #2 pencils with erasers. (ETS)

- Wear a watch. (ETS)

- Eat a light breakfast.

- Bring a scientific calculator. (ETS)

- Select a good seat. Do not sit near anything or anyone that will distract you. You can speak to your friends later.

- If you are easily distracted, bring a pair of earplugs and use them once the test has started.

- Use your test booklet for scratch paper. No one reviews material written on the test booklet.

- Read through the questions slowly and carefully. Think of a probable answer before you look at the multiple-choice selection.

- If you are taking the pencil and paper test, go through the questions and answer those about which you are confident. Take subsequent passes through to answer the rest of the questions with the time remaining. Answer every question; there is no penalty for wrong answers. Note that the CBT (computer-based test) may not allow this strategy.

- For essay portions, start by making an outline in the "notes" space; nothing you write there will be graded. Organize your essay before you begin. The job will be half done before you start. Include a thesis statement, introduction, topic sentence, expansion on the topic, and conclusion. Be sure to double-space your writing so that you can edit if necessary by neatly crossing out and replacing words.

- Keep track of your answers on your answer sheet – make sure you are in the correct sequence. Read topics carefully.

- Stay focused, and do not panic. You are expected to give incorrect answers. Your goal is to pass, not get a perfect score.

Multiple Choice Strategies

- Read the questions carefully. Some words are frequently word traps, including *not, least, except, always,* and *never.* When you see these words, read the question a second time.

- Do not panic if you do not immediately know the answer. Cross off the options that are clearly incorrect, and then reason about the remaining choices. If you took the approach to learning discussed previously, you will be prepared for this ambiguous situation, and be able to find the answer. Reasoning is a virtue; practice it!

- For math questions, do the problem in your head. Cross out answers that are definitely incorrect. Work the problem; you will have already eliminated the "trick" answer.

State-by-State Requirements and Passing Scores

The following chart lists the Web sites that show which Praxis tests are currently required in different states and U.S. territories. Most states are in the norm-referencing phase, and up-to-the minute information can be accessed at www.ets.org/praxis/prxstate.html.

States	State Teacher Certification Contact Website
Alabama	http://www.alsde.edu
Alaska	http://www.eed.state.ak.us/teachercertification/
Arizona	http://ade.state.az.us/
Arkansas	http://arkansased.org/teachers/teachers.html
California	http://www.ctc.ca.gov/
Colorado	http://www.cde.state.co.us/
Connecticut	http://www.state.ct.us/sde/dtl/cert/index.htm
Delaware	http://www.doe.state.de.us/info/certification/
Florida	http://www.fldoe.org/
Georgia	http://www.gapsc.com/
Hawaii	http://www.htsb.org/
Idaho	http://www.sde.idaho.gov/TeacherCertification/default.asp
Illinois	http://www.isbe.state.il.us/
Indiana	http://www.doe.state.in.us/dps/welcome.html
Iowa	http://www.iowa.gov/educate/
Kansas	http://www.ksde.org/Default.aspx?tabid=1648
Kentucky	http://www.kyepsb.net/
Louisiana	http://www.doe.state.la.us/lde/tsac/home.html
Maine	http://www.state.me.us/education/
Maryland	http://www.marylandpublicschools.org/MSDE/divisions/certification/
Massachusetts	http://www.doe.mass.edu/
Michigan	http://www.michigan.gov/mde
Minnesota	http://education.state.mn.us/mde/index.html
Mississippi	http://www.mde.k12.ms.us/ed_licensure/index.html

Missouri	http://dese.mo.gov/divteachqual/teachcert/
Montana	http://www.opi.state.mt.us/
Nebraska	http://www.nde.state.ne.us/tcert/tcmain.html
Nevada	http://ccsd.net/schools/index.phtml
New Hampshire	http://www.ed.state.nh.us/
New Jersey	http://www.state.nj.us/njded/educators/license/
New Mexico	http://sde.state.nm.us/index.html
New York	http://www.highered.nysed.gov/tcert/certificate/
North Carolina	http://www.ncpublicschools.org/
North Dakota	http://governor.state.nd.us/boards/
Ohio	http://www.ode.state.oh.us
Oklahoma	http://sde.state.ok.us/home/defaultie.html
Oregon	http://www.tspc.state.or.us/
Pennsylvania	http://www.pde.state.pa.us/
Rhode Island	http://www.ridoe.net/
South Carolina	http://www.scteachers.org/
South Dakota	http://doe.sd.gov/
Tennessee	http://www.state.tn.us/education/
Texas	http://www.tea.state.tx.us/
Utah	http://www.usoe.k12.ut.us/
Vermont	http://www.state.vt.us/educ/
Virginia	http://www.pen.k12.va.us/
Washington	http://www.k12.wa.us/certification/
District of Columbia	http://www.k12.dc.us/dcps/home.html
West Virginia	http://wvde.state.wv.us/
Wisconsin	http://www.dpi.state.wi.us/dpi/dlsis/tel/licguide.html
Wyoming	http://www.k12.wy.us/

The following chart shows which states currently require the Praxis I tests and the Praxis II pedagogy tests. Most states are in the norm-referencing phase, and up-to-the minute information can be accessed at http://www.ets.org/praxis/prxstate.html.

State	10710 PPST Reading	20720 PPST Writing	10730 PPST Math	30521 Early Childhood	30522 Grades K-6	30523 Grades 5-9	30524 Grades 7-12
AL	•	•	•				
AK	•	•	•	•		•	•
AZ							
AR	•	•	•		•	•	•
CA							
CO							
CT	•	•	•				
DE	•	•	•				
DC	•	•	•				
FL							
GA						•	
Guam	•	•	•				
HI	•	•	•	•	•	•	•
ID					•	•	
IL							
IN	•	•	•				
IA							
KS				•	•	•	•
KY	•	•	•		•	•	•
LA	•	•	•		•	•	•
ME	•	•	•		•		•
MD	•	•	•	•			•
MA							
MI							
MN	•	•	•	•	•	•	•
MS	•	•	•		•	•	•
MO						•	•
MT							
NE	•	•	•				

NV	•	•	•		•		•
NH	•	•	•				
NJ							
NM							
NY							
NC	•	•	•				
ND	•	•	•		•		
OH	•	•	•	•	•	•	•
OK	•	•	•				
OR	•	•	•				
PA	•	•	•				
RI					•		•
SC	•	•	•		•	•	•
SD				•	•	•	•
TN	•	•	•	•	•	•	•
TX							
US Virgin Islands	•	•	•		•		
UT				•	•	•	•
VT	•	•	•				
VA	•	•	•				
WA							
WV	•	•	•		•	•	•
WI	•	•	•				
WY						•	•

Integration of INTASC Standards with Text Chapters	
INTASC - Interstate New Teachers Assessment and Support Consortium	**TEXT:** *Educational Psychology: Theory and Practice, 9/e* Slavin (2008)
Standard 1 – *Knowledge of Subject Matter* The teacher understands the central concepts, tools of inquiry, and structures of the discipline(s) he or she teaches and can create learning experiences that make these aspects of subject matter meaningful for students.	**Chapter 1**: Educational Psychology
Standard 2 – *Knowledge of Human Development and Learning* The teacher understands how children learn and develop, and can provide learning opportunities that support their intellectual, social and personal development.	**Chapter 2**: Behavioral Learning Theories; **Chapter 3**: Development During Childhood and Adolescence; **Chapter 4**: Student Diversity; **Chapter 5**: Behavioral Theories of Learning; **Chapter 6**: Information Processing and Cognitive Theories of Learning; **Chapter 7**: The Effective Lesson; **Chapter 10**: Motivating Students to Learn; **Chapter 12:** Learners with Exceptionalities
Standard 3 – *Adapting Instruction for Individual Needs* The teacher understands how students differ in their approaches to learning and creates instructional opportunities that are adapted to diverse learners.	**Chapter 1**: Educational Psychology: A Foundation for Teaching; **Chapter 2**: Theories of Development; **Chapter 3**: Development During Childhood and Adolescence; **Chapter 4**: Student Diversity; **Chapter 5**: Behavioral Theories of Learning; **Chapter 6**: Information Processing and Cognitive Theories of Learning; **Chapter 8**: Student-Centered and Constructivist Approaches to Instruction; **Chapter 9**: Accommodating Instruction to Meet Individual Needs; **Chapter 10**: Motivating Students to Learn; **Chapter 12:** Learners with Exceptionalities
Standard 4 – *Multiple Instructional Strategies* The teacher understands and uses a variety of instructional strategies to encourage students' development of critical thinking, problem solving, and performance skills.	**Chapter 2**: Theories of Development; **Chapter 4**: Student Diversity; **Chapter 5**: Behavioral Theories of Learning; **Chapter 6**: Information Processing and Cognitive Theories of Learning; **Chapter 7**: The Effective Lesson; **Chapter 8**: Student-Centered and Constructivist Approaches to Instruction; **Chapter 10**: Motivating Students to Learn; **Chapter 11**: Effective Learning Environments; **Chapter 12:** Learners with Exceptionalities
Standard 5 – *Classroom Motivation and Management* The teacher uses an understanding of individual and group motivation and behavior to create a learning environment that encourages positive social interaction, active engagement in learning, and self-motivation	**Chapter 1**: Educational Psychology; **Chapter 4**: Student Diversity ; **Chapter 7**: The Effective Lesson; **Chapter 8**: Student-Centered and Constructivist Approaches to Instruction; **Chapter 9**: Accommodating Instruction to Meet Individual Needs; **Chapter 10**: Motivating Students to Learn; **Chapter 11**: Effective Learning Environments; **Chapter 12:** Learners with Exceptionalities ; **Chapter 13**: Assessing Student Learning

Standard 6 – *Communication Skills* The teacher uses knowledge of effective verbal, nonverbal, and media communication techniques to foster active inquiry, collaboration, and supportive interaction in the classroom.	**Chapter 4**: Student Diversity ; **Chapter 6**: Information Processing and Cognitive Theories of Learning; **Chapter 7**: The Effective Lesson; **Chapter 9**: Accommodating Instruction to Meet Individual Needs; **Chapter 11**: Effective Learning Environments; **Chapter 12**: Learners with Exceptionalities ; **Chapter 13**: Assessing Student Learning
Standard 7 – *Instructional Planning Skills* The teacher plans instruction based upon knowledge of subject matter, students, the community, and curriculum goals.	**Chapter 1**: Educational Psychology: A Foundation for Teaching; **Chapter 3**: Development During Childhood and Adolescence; **Chapter 4**: Student Diversity; **Chapter 7**: The Effective Lesson; **Chapter 8**: Student-Centered and Constructivist Approaches to Instruction; **Chapter 9**: Accommodating Instruction to Meet Individual Needs; **Chapter 10**: Motivating Students to Learn; **Chapter 11**: Effective Learning Environments; **Chapter 12**: Learners with Exceptionalities; **Chapter 13**: Assessing Student Learning; **Chapter 14**: Standardized Tests and Accountability
Standard 8 – *Assessment of Student Learning* The teacher understands and uses formal and informal assessment strategies to evaluate and ensure the continuous intellectual, social and physical development of the learner.	**Every Chapter**
Standard 9 - *Professional Commitment and Responsibility* The teacher is a reflective practitioner who continually evaluates the effects of his/her choices and actions on others (students, parents, and other professionals in the learning community) and who actively seeks out opportunities to grow professionally.	**Every Chapter**
Standard 10 – *Partnerships* The teacher fosters relationships with school colleagues, parents, and agencies in the larger community to support students' learning and well-being.	**Chapter 3**: Development During Childhood and Adolescence; **Chapter 4**: Student Diversity; **Chapter 9**: Accommodating Instruction to Meet Individual Needs; **Chapter 11**: Effective Learning Environments; **Chapter 12**: Learners with Exceptionalities

SECTION 2: CORRELATIONS TO THE TEXTBOOK

General Information about Educational Psychology

What is educational psychology? According to your textbook author Robert Slavin, educational psychology is defined as the accumulated knowledge, wisdom, and seat-of-the pants theory that every teacher should possess to intelligently solve the daily problems of teaching. Educational psychology cannot tell teachers what to do, but it can give them the principles to use in making a good decision and a language to discuss their experiences and thinking (p. 3).

For the Praxis II pedagogy tests, you will be expected to know theories, theorists, and operational terms that represent what is currently known about educational psychology. You will be expected to apply these theories to case histories and scenario readings.

Demonstrating Potential for Teaching Expertise and the Praxis II

The Praxis II tests your potential to become an expert teacher, by using case histories and short answer questions to assess working knowledge. According to the *Test at a Glance Guide* for the *Principles of Learning and Teaching* assessments (0521, 0522, 0523, & 0524), short answer questions require the examinee to:

> *"demonstrate understanding of the importance of an aspect of teaching, demonstrate understanding of principles of learning and teaching underlying an aspect of teaching, or recognize when and how to apply the principles of learning and teaching underlying an aspect of teaching." (p. 10)*

An example of a case history found on the Praxis II Principles of Learning and Teaching, can be found on page 5 of the *Test at a Glance* document for test 0523, grades 5-9. (Go to the following website to download this Test at a Glance and others: www.ets.org/praxis/prxtest.html. If you do not already have Acrobat reader, you can download it at the ETS site). In this example, the case of Mr. Jenner, a second-year teacher beginning his fourth week of instruction, is presented. Documentation includes Mr. Jenner's project plan, a supervisor's observation notes and transcripts, and transcripts of a conversation between Mr. Jenner and a colleague. Sample questions follow the case history, along with a scoring guide. Scores range from 0 to 2, with a score of 0 indicating no appropriate responses to any part of the question, a score of 1 representing an answer with appropriate responses to part of the question, and a score of 2 representing an answer with appropriate responses to all parts of the question, along with demonstration of understanding of both the case history and the principles of learning and teaching outlined in the content categories covered in the test (p. 8). The *Test at a Glance* also presents two sample questions, along with responses to each representing scores of 0, 1, and 2. Below is the second sample question, along with a discussion of the sample responses receiving scores of 0, 1, and 2. The actual sample test questions can be found on page 9 of the *Test at a Glance* (0523).

Question 2. Review the assessment section of Mr. Jenner's Project Plan. Explain TWO ways Mr. Jenner could strengthen this section to help students have a better opportunity to demonstrate their accomplishments in this project. Base your response on principles of formal and informal assessment.

Mr. Jenner's Project Plan taken directly from page 5, *Test at a Glance* (0523).
World Cultures Panel Presentation

Objectives: Students will
1. Review and use concepts about world cultures
2. Demonstrate speaking and listening skills
3. Use creativity (art, literature, music, multimedia, objects)
4. Use higher-order thinking skills

Assignment:
1. You will work in assigned groups of five
2. Each group will select one culture from a list
3. The group will plan, gather information, and present a panel report to the class on the culture
4. Use the characteristics of a culture studied last week to organize your presentation
5. Include some use of art, literature, music, multimedia, or other cultural objects
6. All students must participate in group planning and presentation

Activities:
1. Presentation/discussion of assignment; video of effective panel from another class; assign groups
2. Group work: select culture; plan presentation, assign responsibilities
3. Group work: prepare presentations
4. Panel presentations
5. Writing assignment: comparison/contrast of cultures

Assessment:
1. Group work: individual and group grade
2. Panel presentation: individual and group grade
3. Writing assignment

Let us begin with a sample response receiving a score of 0. Although the *Test At A Glance* presents the highest score first, we will to build up to the best; it gives us something to look forward to! The sample responses are taken directly from page 9 of the *Test at a Glance* (0523).

Sample response receiving a score 0: He could add a reading assignment. It looks like students are going to just do the work and share all their ideas. But they would do a much better job if he assigned some reading, so that they would have more information to draw on. This would help strengthen the knowledge about cultures that they have.

Critique:

Definitions of formal and informal assessment. According to Slavin, "Assessment is a measure of the degree to which instructional objectives have been attained. Because instructional objectives are stated in terms of how they will be measured, it is clear that objectives are closely linked to assessment. Most assessments in schools are tests or quizzes, or informal verbal assessment such as questions in class. However, students can also show their learning by writing an essay, painting a picture, doing a car tune-up, or baking a pineapple upside-down cake" (p. 446).

Looking back at the scoring criteria, a high score of 2 demands that the response answers the question asked. This response does not respond to the question being asked. Instead of focusing on the assessment criteria, the respondent focuses on the assignment. Further, the suggestion demonstrates poor understanding of the project plan. The assignment includes information gathering as a key component of the project. Further, the respondent addresses "strengthening student knowledge," an issue not addressed in the question. In essence, this is a poor answer because the respondent did not respond to the questions being asked. A good result requires that you read the question carefully, and organize your response to respond to each part of the question. Let's look at the next sample response.

Sample response receiving a score 1: He could add another assessment toward the beginning to be sure students begin to understand what an effective panel is. Before showing the video of the panel, he could tell students that as soon as it is over, they are to explain what they saw that they thought was effective. This would assess both their viewing and listening skills and their ability to figure out what effective panels are.

Critique:

Clearly this is a better response than the first. However, it receives a score of 1 because the respondent provided only one solution, not two as requested. Further, although the respondent provided a fine example of a formal assessment, including attention to both viewing and listening skills, the proposed addition assesses knowledge pertaining to how a panel works, whereas the question clearly asks for suggestions strengthening Mr. Jenner's assessment of student accomplishment in the project, not knowledge of how a panel works. Although some may feel it is picky, it is best to follow verbatim questions asked, and answer as tightly all the question content as possible.

Sample response receiving a score 2: The best for last!

- Add an indication of the criteria on which each assessment will be made - students need to know more than the names or kinds of assessments - they need to know on what their work will be evaluated.
- Add an assessment at the end, so each student has an opportunity to demonstrate what has been learned, either about all the cultures reported on or about the specific culture the student studied.

Critique: This response deserves a 2 because it answers the question in total. First, it provides two ways Mr. Jenner could strengthen the assessment section. Second, the response stays within the parameters of the question. Recall that the question asked for two ways to strengthen the assessment section to help students demonstrate their accomplishments. The response provides two ways. First, Mr. Jenner should provide more information on how student work will be evaluated. This suggestion provides more information for students to craft an appropriate response. Providing criterion in advance alleviates anxiety from confusion about grading standards. For more information about different types of grading, see page 450 of the Fetsco and McClure text.

The second suggestion refers to an objective assessment of student knowledge of the cultures covered in panel reports. This assessment supports knowledge attained in activity 5, comparing and contrasting cultures. Further, it helps focus student attention by providing an additional criterion, and motivates students with an extrinsic reward.

Overall, this response is a good response because it answers all parts of the question asked, and demonstrates understanding of the case study, as shown in the last paragraph. Further, the response demonstrates understanding of the topics covered on the test, including topic II, section C, page 12, Assessment Strategies.

Discrete multiple-choice questions

The remaining questions in the Praxis II Principles of Learning and Teaching series (0522-0524) are multiple-choice items assessing conceptual knowledge. They do not relate to the earlier case studies, but still test working knowledge. The first suggestion is for you study your textbook thoroughly, reviewing the key theories and concepts in preparation for the test. Go back to **Section 1: General Praxis Test Information**, and review the **test taking tips**. Also, be sure to familiarize yourself with the vocabulary below, and play with the terms mentally, applying concepts learned in class and textbooks to real situations. For instance, many students have trouble understanding the concept of *negative reinforcement*. Essentially, they do not understand why negative reinforcement is just as likely as positive reinforcement to increase the likelihood of behavioral repetition. After all, how can something negative be positive? To appreciate the concept of negative reinforcement, you can evaluate daily activities for examples of positive and negative reinforcement. If, for example, you like calling home and speaking to your mom when you are feeling down, you have experienced a negatively reinforcing event. If calling mom lifted your spirits, removing displeasure, the call was a negatively reinforcing event; it removed something that was not pleasant. Removing something unpleasant is just as reinforcing as adding something pleasant, isn't it? Life is filled with such simple examples of concepts learned in educational psychology; you just have to open your eyes to see them. Once you see them, your conceptual understanding will improve exponentially! Further, the better you can apply your knowledge to actual situations, the more likely will you be able to apply it to counterfactual situations encountered during a test like the Praxis. So **PRAX**TICE makes perfect!

Vocabulary Drill Sheets

As mentioned in the first section, creating vocabulary drill cards and notecards can help you remember educational psychology terms and facts for the Praxis II pedagogy tests. They can also help you with the case studies and provide you with content for your essays.

Fold the following pages in half, with the terms on one side and the definitions on the other. Have a friend quiz you on the meanings of the words. Mark the ones you don't know for future additional study. You can also do this by yourself: just look at the side with the terms, and provide a definition before turning over the paper to check your answer. As an additional incentive to learn these terms, try coming up with a definition in your own words and an example using the term.

Acceleration programs	Rapid promotion through advanced studies for students who are gifted or talented.
Accommodation	Modifying existing schemes to fit new situations (Piaget).
Accountability	The degree to which people are held responsible for their task performances or decision outcomes.
Achievement batteries	Standardized tests that include several subtests designed to measure knowledge of particular subtests.
Achievement motivation	The desire to experience success and to participate in activities in which success depends on personal effort and abilities.
Achievement tests	Standardized tests measuring how much students have learned in a given context.
Action research	Research carried out by educators in their own classrooms or schools.
Adaptation	The process of adjusting schemes in response to the environment by means of assimilation and accommodation (Piaget).

Advance organizers	Activities and techniques that orient students to the material before reading or class presentation.
Affective objectives	Objectives that have to do with student attitudes and values.
Allocated time	Time during which students have the opportunity to learn.
Analogies	Images, concepts, or narratives that compare new information to information students already understand.
Antecedent stimuli	Events that precede behaviors.
Applied behavior analysis	The application of behavioral learning principles to understanding and changing behavior.
Aptitude test	A test designed to measure general abilities and to predict future performance.
Aptitude-treatment interaction	Interaction of individual differences in learning with particular teaching methods.
Assertive Discipline	Method of giving clear, firm, unhostile response to student misbehavior.
Assessment	A measure of the degree to which instructional objectives have been attained.
Assimilation	Understanding new experiences in terms of existing schemes (Piaget).
Associative play	Play that is much like parallel play but with increased levels of interaction in the form of sharing, turn-taking, and general interest in what others are doing.

Attention

Active focus on certain stimuli to the exclusion of others.

Attention Deficit Hyperactivity Disorder

ADHD: A disorder characterized by difficulties maintaining attention because of a limited ability to concentrate; includes impulsive actions and hyperactive behavior.

Attribution theory

A theory of motivation that focuses on how people explain the causes of their own successes and failures.

Autism

A category of disability that significantly affects social interaction, verbal and nonverbal communication, and educational performance.

Autism spectrum disorder

A broad range of severity, including a mild form of Autism called Asperger's Syndrome.

Automaticity

A level of rapidity and ease such that tasks can be performed or skills utilized with little mental effort.

Autonomous Morality

In Piaget's theory of moral development, the stage at which a person understands that people make rules and that punishments are not automatic.

Aversive stimulus

An unpleasant consequence that a person tries to avoid or escape.

Backward planning

Planning instruction by first setting long-range goals, then setting unit objectives, and finally planning daily lessons.

Behavioral learning theories

Explanations of learning that emphasize observable changes in behavior.

Behavior content matrix	A chart that classifies lesson objectives according to cognitive level.
Behavior modification	Systematic application of antecedents and consequences to change behavior.
Between-class ability grouping	The practice of grouping students in separate classes according to ability level.
Bias	An undesirable characteristic of tests in which item content discriminates against certain students.
Bilingual education	Instructional program for students who speak little or no English in which some instruction is provided in the native language.
Calling order	The order in which students are called on by the teacher to answer questions during the course of a lesson.
CD-ROM	A computer database designed for "read-only memory" that provides massive amounts of information, including pictures and audio; it can be of particular importance to students doing projects and research activities.
Centration	Paying attention to only one aspect of an object or situation (Piaget).
Choral responses	Responses to questions made by an entire class in unison.
Chronological age	The age of an individual in years.
Clang	Features that make a choice stand out in multiple-choice questions.

Class inclusion

A skill learned during the concrete operational stage of cognitive development in which individuals can think simultaneously about a whole class of objects and about relationships among its subordinate classes (Piaget).

Classical Conditioning

The process of repeatedly associating a previously neutral stimulus with an unconditioned stimulus in order to evoke a conditioned response.

Classroom management

Methods used to organize classroom activities, instruction, physical structure, and other features to make effective use of time, to create a happy and productive learning environment, and to minimize behavior problems and other disruptions.

Cognitive apprenticeship

The process by which a learner gradually acquires expertise through interaction with an expert, either an adult or an older or more advanced peer.

Cognitive behavior modification

Procedures based on both behavioral and cognitive principles for changing one's own behavior by means of self-talk and self-instruction (e.g., Meichenbaum).

Cognitive development

Gradual, orderly changes by which mental processes become more complex and sophisticated.

Cognitive Learning theories

Explanations of learning that focus on mental processes.

Collaboration

Process in which professionals work cooperatively to provide educational services.

Compensatory education	Programs designed to prevent or remediate learning problems among students from lower socioeconomic status communities.
Compensatory Preschool Programs	Programs that are designed to prepare disadvantaged children for entry into kindergarten and first grade.
Completion items	Fill-in-the-blank test items.
Computer-adaptive	An approach to assessment in which a computer is used to present items and each item presented is chosen to yield the best new information about the examinee based on her or his prior responses to earlier items.
Computer-assisted instruction (CAI)	Individualized instruction administered by computer.
Computer programming	Creating instructions for a computer to perform specific functions.
Concept	An abstract idea that is generalized from specific examples.
Concurrent evidence	A type of criterion-related evidence of validity that exists when scores on a test are related to scores from another measure of the same or a very similar trait.
Concrete Operational Stage	Stage at which children develop the capacity for logical reasoning and understanding of conservation but can use these skills only in dealing with familiar situations (Piaget).
Conditioned stimulus	A previously neutral stimulus that evokes a particular response after having been paired with an unconditioned stimulus.

Conduct disorders

Socioemotional and behavioral disorders that are indicated in individuals who, for example, are chronically disobedient or disruptive.

Consequences

Pleasant or unpleasant conditions that follow behaviors and affect the frequency of future behaviors.

Conservation

The concept that certain properties of an object (such as weight) remain the same regardless of changes in other properties (such as length) (Piaget).

Constructivism

View of cognitive development that emphasizes the active role of learners in building their understanding of reality.

Constructivist theories of learning

Theories that state that learners must individually discover and transform complex information, checking new information against old rules and revising rules when they no longer work.

Content evidence

A measure of the match between the content of a test and the content of the instruction that preceded it.

Content integration

Teachers' use of examples, data, and other information from a variety of cultures.

Contingent praise

Praise that is effective because it refers directly to specific task performances.

Continuous theory of development

Theory based on the belief that human development progresses smoothly and gradually from infancy to adulthood.

Control group

Group that receives no special treatment during an experiment.

Conventional Level of Morality	Stages 3 and 4 in Kohlberg's model of moral reasoning, in which individuals make moral judgments in consideration of others.
Cooperative Integrated Reading and Composition	A comprehensive program for teaching reading and writing in the upper elementary grades; students work in four-member cooperative learning teams. [CIRC]
Cooperative learning	Instructional approaches in which students work in small mixed-ability groups.
Cooperative play	Play in which children join together to achieve a common goal.
Cooperative scripting	A study method in which students work in pairs and take turns orally summarizing sections of material to be learned.
Correlational study	Research into the relationship between variables as they naturally occur.
Criterion-related evidence	A type of evidence of validity that exists when scores on a test are related to scores from another measure of an associated trait.
Criterion-referenced interpretations	Assessments that rate how thoroughly students have mastered specific skills or areas of knowledge.
Critical thinking	Evaluation of conclusions through logical and systematic examination of the problem, the evidence, and the solution.
Cross-age tutoring	Tutoring of a younger student by an older one.
Cues	Signals as to what behavior(s) will be reinforced or punished.

Culture
The language, attitudes, ways of behaving, and other aspects of life that characterize a group of people.

Cutoff score
The score designated as the minimum necessary to demonstrate mastery of the subject.

Databases
Computer programs that contain large volumes of information, such as encyclopedias and atlases.

Deficiency needs
Basic requirements for physical and psychological well-being as identified by Maslow.

Derived scores
Values computed from raw scores that relate students' performances to those of a norming group, e.g., percentiles and grade equivalents.

Desktop publishing
A computer application for writing compositions that lends itself to revising and editing.

Descriptive research
Research study aimed at identifying and gathering detailed information about something of interest.

Development
Orderly and lasting growth, adaptation, and change over the course of a lifetime.

Developmentally appropriate education
Instruction felt to be adapted to the current developmental status of children (rather than of their age alone).

Diagnostic tests
Tests of specific skills used to identify students' needs and to guide instruction.

Digital photographs
Photographs that can be loaded into a computer and shared electronically.

Direct instruction	Approach to teaching in which the teacher transmits information directly to the students; lessons are goal-oriented and structured by the teacher.
Disability	The limitation of a function, such as cognitive processing or physical or sensory abilities.
Discipline	Methods used to prevent behavior problems from occurring or to respond to behavior problems so as to reduce their recurrence in the future.
Discontinuous theories of development	Theories describing human development as occurring through a fixed sequence of distinct, predictable stages governed by inborn factors.
Discovery learning	A constructivist approach to teaching in which students are encouraged to discover principles for themselves.
Discriminant evidence	A type of evidence of validity that exists when scores on a test are unrelated to scores from one or more measures of other traits when educational or psychological theory about these traits predicts they should be unrelated.
Discrimination	Perception of and response to differences in stimuli.
Distractors	Incorrect responses that are offered as alternative answers to a multiple-choice question.
Distributed practice	Technique in which items to be learned are repeated at intervals over a period of time.

Drill-and-practice	Application of computer technology to provide students with practice of skills and knowledge.
Dual Code Theory of Memory	Theory suggesting that information coded both visually and verbally is remembered better than information coded in only one of those two ways.
Early intervention	Programs that target at-risk infants and toddlers to prevent possible later need for remediation.
Early intervention programs	Compensatory preschool programs that target very young children at the greatest risk of school failure.
Educational Psychology	The study of learning and teaching.
Egocentric	Believing that everyone views the world as you do (Piaget).
Elaboration	The process of connecting new material to information or ideas already in the learner's mind.
Embedded multimedia	Video content woven into teachers' lessons
Emergent Literacy	Knowledge and skills relating to reading that children usually develop from experience with books and other print media before the beginning of formal reading instruction in school.
Emotional and behavioral disorders	Exceptionalities characterized by problems with learning, interpersonal relationships, and control of feelings and behaviors.
Empowering school culture	A school culture in which the institution's organization and practices are conducive to the academic and emotional growth of all students.

Enactment	A learning process in which individuals physically carry out tasks.
Engaged time or time-on-task	Time students spend actually learning; same as *time-on-task*.
English as a Second Language (ESL)	Subject taught in English classes and programs for students who are not native speakers of English.
Enrichment activities	Assignments or activities designed to broaden or deepen the knowledge of students who master classroom lessons quickly.
Enrichment programs	Programs in which assignments or activities are designed to broaden or deepen the knowledge of students who master classroom lessons quickly.
Episodic memory	A part of long-term memory that stores images of our personal experiences.
Equilibration	The process of restoring balance between present understanding and new experiences (Piaget).
Equity pedagogy	Teaching techniques that facilitate the academic success of students from different ethnic and social class groups.
Ethnic group	A group within a larger society that sees itself as having a common history, social and cultural heritage, and traditions, often based on race, religion, language, or national identity.
Ethnicity	A history, culture, and sense of identity shared by a group of people.

Evaluation	Measurement of student performance in academic and, sometimes, other areas; used to determine appropriate teaching strategies.
Evaluative descriptors	Statements describing strong and weak features of a response to an item, a question, or a project.
Expectancy theory	A theory of motivation based on the belief that people's efforts to achieve depend on their expectations of reward.
Expectancy-valence model	A theory that relates the probability and the incentive value of success to motivation.
Experiment	Procedure used to test the effect of a treatment.
Experimental group	Group that receives treatment during an experiment.
External validity	Degree to which results of an experiment can be applied to real-life situations.
Extinction	The weakening and eventual elimination of a learned behavior as reinforcement is withdrawn.
Extinction burst	The increase in levels of a behavior in the early stages of extinction.
Extrinsic incentive	A reward that is external to the activity, such as recognition or a good grade.
Extrinsic reinforcers	Praise or rewards given to motivate people to engage in behavior that they might not engage in without them.
Feedback	Information on the results of one's efforts.

Fixed-Interval schedule	Reinforcement schedule in which desired behavior is rewarded following a constant amount of time.
Fixed-Ratio (FR) schedule	Reinforcement schedule in which a desired behavior is rewarded following a fixed number of behaviors.
Flashbulb memory	Important events that are fixed mainly in visual and auditory memory.
Foreclosure	An adolescent's premature establishment of an identity based on parental choices, not on his or her own.
Formal Operational Stage	Stage at which one can deal abstractly with hypothetical situations and can reason logically (Piaget).
Formative assessment	Evaluations designed to determine whether additional instruction is needed.
Free-recall learning	Learning of a list of items in any order.
Full inclusion	Arrangement whereby students who have disabilities or are at risk receive all their instruction in a general education setting; support services are brought to the student.
Gender bias	Stereotypical views and differential treatment of males and females, often favoring one gender over the other.
Generalization	Carry-over of behaviors, skills, or concepts from one setting or task to another.

Giftedness	Exceptional intellectual ability, creativity, or talent.
Grade-equivalent scores	Standard scores that relate students' raw scores to the average scores obtained by norming groups at different grade levels.
Group alerting	Questioning strategies that encourage all students to pay attention during lectures and discussions.
Group contingencies	Class rewards that depend on the behavior of all students.
Group contingency program	A program in which rewards or punishments are given to a class as a whole for adhering to or violating rules of conduct.
Group Investigation	A cooperative learning model in which students work in small groups using cooperative inquiry, group discussion, and cooperative planning and projects, and then make presentations to the whole class on their findings.
Growth needs	Needs for knowing, appreciating, and understanding, which people try to satisfy after their basic needs are met (Maslow).
Halo effect	Bias due to carryover of a general attitude about a respondent, as when a teacher knows which student wrote which response and alters the grading depending on his or her opinion of the student.
Handicap	A conditioned imposed on a person with disabilities by society, the physical environment, or the person's attitude.

Hearing disabilities	Degree of deafness; uncorrectable inability to hear well.
Heteronomous Morality	In Piaget's theory of moral development, the stage at which children think that rules are unchangeable and that breaking them leads automatically to punishment.
Home-based reinforcement strategies	Behavior modification strategies in which a student's school behavior is reported to parents, who supply rewards.
Hypertext and hypermedia	Related information that appears when a computer user clicks on a word or picture.
Identity achievement	A state of consolidation reflecting conscious, clear-cut decisions concerning occupation and ideology.
Identity diffusion	Inability to develop a clear direction or sense of self.
Imagery	Mental visualization of images to improve memory.
Independent practice	Component of instruction in which students work by themselves to demonstrate and rehearse new knowledge.
Individualized Education Program (IEP)	A program tailored to the needs of the learner with exceptionalities.
Individualized instruction	Instruction tailored to particular students' needs, in which each student works at his or her own level and rate.
Individuals with Disabilities Education Act	P.L. 101-476, a federal law enacted in 1990 that changed the name of P.L. 94-142 and broadened services to adolescents with disabilities. (IDEA)

Inert knowledge

Learned information that could be applied to a wide range of situations but whose use is limited to restricted, often artificial applications.

Inferred reality

The meaning of stimuli in the context of relevant information (Piaget).

Information-Processing Theory

Cognitive theory of learning that describes the processing, storage, and retrieval of knowledge in the mind.

Interactive whiteboard

An interactive display surface that makes it possible to save to a computer file, edit, and print notes or illustrations that have been written on it.

Initial-letter strategies

Strategies for learning in which initial letters of items to be memorized are made into a more easily remembered word or phrase.

Instructional games

Drill and practice exercises presented in a game format.

Instructional objective

A statement of skills or concepts students should master after a given period of instruction.

Instrumental Enrichment

A thinking skills program in which students work through a series of paper-and-pencil exercises that are designed to develop various intellectual abilities.

Integrated learning systems

Commercially developed comprehensive, multipurpose packages of interlinked management instructional software, running on a computer network.

Intelligence	General aptitude for learning, often measured by the ability to deal with abstractions and to solve problems.
Intelligence quotient (IQ)	An intelligence test score that should be near 100 for people of average intelligence.
Intentionality	Doing things for a purpose; teachers who use intentionality plan their actions based on the outcomes they want to achieve.
Interference	Inhibition of recall of certain information by the presence of other information in memory.
Internal validity	The degree to which an experiment's results can be attributed to the treatment in question, not to other factors.
Internet	A large and growing telecommunications network of computers around the world that communicate electronically.
Intrinsic incentive	An aspect of an activity that people enjoy and therefore find motivating.
Intrinsic reinforcers	Behaviors that a person enjoys engaging in for their own sake, without any other reward.
Jigsaw	A cooperative learning model in which students are assigned to six-member teams to work on academic material that has been broken down into sections for each member.
Joplin Plan	A regrouping method in which students are grouped across grade lines for reading instruction.
Keyword method	A strategy for improving memory by using images to link pairs of items.

Knowledge construction	Helping students understand how the knowledge we take in is influenced by our origins and points of view.
Laboratory experiment	Experiment in which conditions are highly controlled.
Language disorders	Impairments in one's ability to understand language or to express ideas in one's native language.
Language minority	In the United States, native speakers of any language other than English.
Large muscle development	Development of motor skills such as running or throwing, which involve the limbs and large muscles.
Learned helplessness	The expectation, based on experience, that one's actions will ultimately lead to failure.
Learner with exceptionalities	Any individual whose physical, mental, or behavioral performance is so different from the norm – either higher or lower – that special services are needed to meet the individual's needs.
Learning	A change in an individual that results from experience.
Learning disabilities (LD)	Disorders that impede academic progress of people who are not mentally retarded or emotionally disturbed.
Learning or mastery goals	The goals of students who are motivated primarily by desire for knowledge acquisition and self-improvement. Also called mastery goals.
Learning objectives	Specific behaviors that students are expected to exhibit at the end of a series of lessons.

Learning Together	A cooperative learning model in which students in four-or-five member heterogeneous groups work together on assignments.
Learning probe	A method, such as questioning, that helps teachers find out whether students understand a lesson.
Learning styles	Orientations for approaching learning tasks and processing information in certain ways.
Least restrictive environment	Provision in IDEA that requires students with disabilities to be educated with nondisabled peers to the maximum extent appropriate. (LRE)
Lesson planning	Procedure that includes stating learning objectives such as what the students should know or be able to do after the lesson; what information, activities, and experiences the teacher will provide; how much time will be needed to reach the objective; what books, materials, and media support the teacher will provide; and what instructional method(s) and participation structures will be used.
Levels-of-Processing Theory	Explanation of memory that links recall of a stimulus with the amount of mental processing it receives.
Limited English Proficient (LEP)	Possessing limited mastery of English.
Loci method	A strategy for remembering lists by picturing items in familiar locations.
Locus of control	A personality trait that determines whether people attribute responsibility for their own failure or success to internal or external factors.

Long essay item

A test question requiring an answer of more than a page.

Long-term memory

The components of memory in which large amounts of information can be stored for long periods of time.

Mainstreaming

The temporal, instructional, and social integration of eligible children with exceptionalities with peers without exceptionalities based on an ongoing, individually determined educational planning and programming process.

Maintenance

Continuation (of behavior).

Mapping

Diagramming main ideas and the connections between them.

Massed practice

Technique in which facts or skills to be learned are repeated often over a concentrated period of time.

Mastery grading

Grading requiring an established standard of mastery, such as 80 or 90 percent correct on a test. Students who do not achieve it the first time may receive corrective instruction and then retake the test to try to achieve mastery.

Matching items

Test items that are presented in two lists, each item in one list matching one or more items in the other list.

Meaningful learning

Mental processing of new information that relates to previously learned knowledge.

Means-end analysis

A problem-solving technique that encourages identifying the goal(ends) to be attained, the current situation, and what needs to be done(means) to reduce the difference between the two conditions.

Mediated learning	Assisted learning; an approach in which the teacher guides instruction by means of scaffolding to help students master and internalize the skills that permit higher cognitive functioning.
Mental retardation	A condition, usually present at birth, that results in below-average intellectual skills and poor adaptive behavior.
Mental age	The average test score received by individuals of a given chronological age.
Mental set	Students' attitude of readiness to begin a lesson.
Metacognition	Knowledge about one's own learning or about how to learn ("thinking about thinking").
Metacognitive skills	Methods for learning, studying, or solving problems.
Minority group	An ethnic or racial group that is a minority within a broader population.
Mnemonics	Devices or strategies for aiding the memory.
Mock participation	Situation in which students appear to be on-task but are not engaged in learning.
Modeling	Imitation of other's behavior.
Moral dilemmas	In Kohlberg's theory of moral reasoning, hypothetical situations that require a person to consider values of right and wrong.

Moratorium	Experimentation with occupational and ideological choices without definite commitment.
Motivation	The influence of needs and desires on the intensity and direction of behavior.
Multicultural education	Education that teaches the value of cultural diversity.
Multifactor aptitude battery	A test that predicts ability to learn a variety of specific skills and types of knowledge.
Multimedia	Electronic material such as graphics, video, animation, and sound, which can be integrated into classroom projects.
Multiple-choice items	Test items that usually consist of a stem followed by choices or alternatives.
Multiple intelligences	In Gardner's theory of intelligence, a person's eight separate abilities; logical/mathematical, linguistic, musical, naturalist, spatial, bodily/kinesthetic, interpersonal, and intrapersonal.
Negative correlation	Relationship in which high levels of one variable correspond to low levels of another.
Negative reinforcer	Release from an unpleasant situation, given to strengthen behavior.
Neutral stimuli	Stimuli that have no effect on a particular response.
Nongraded programs	Programs, generally at the primary level, that combine children of different ages in the same class. Also called *cross-age grouping programs*.

Nonverbal cues

Eye contact, gestures, physical proximity, or touching that a teacher uses to communicate without interrupting verbal discourse.

Normal curve equivalent

A set of standard scores ranging from 1 to 99, having a mean of 50 and a standard deviation of about 21.

Normal distribution

A bell-shaped symmetrical distribution of scores in which most scores fall near the mean, with progressively fewer occurring as the distance from the mean increases.

Norm-referenced interpretations

Assessments that compare the performance of one student against the performance of others.

Norms

Standards that are derived from the test scores of a sample of people who are similar to those who will take the test and that can be used to interpret scores of future test takers.

Note-taking

A study strategy that requires decisions about what to write.

Object permanence

The fact that an object exists even if it is out of sight (Piaget).

Observational Learning

Learning by observation and imitation of others (Bandura).

Operant Conditioning

The use of pleasant or unpleasant consequences to control the occurrence of behavior.

Outlining

Representing the main points of material in hierarchical format.

Overlapping

A teacher's ability to respond to behavior problems without interrupting a classroom lesson.

Paired-associate learning	Learning of items in linked pairs so that when one member of a pair is presented, the other can be recalled.
Parallel play	Play in which children engage in the same activity side by side but with very little interaction or mutual influence.
Pedagogy	The study of teaching and learning with applications to the instructional process.
Peer tutoring	Tutoring of one student by another.
Peers	People who are equal in age or status.
Pegword method	A strategy for memorization in which images are used to link lists of facts to a familiar set of words or numbers.
Percentile score	A derived score that designates what percentage of the norming group earned raw scores lower than a particular score.
Perception	A person's interpretation of stimuli.
Performance assessments	Assessments of students' ability to perform tasks in real-life contexts, not just to show knowledge. Also called *authentic assessments*.
Performance goals	The goals of students who are motivated primarily by a desire to gain recognition from others and to earn good grades.
Portfolio assessment	Assessment of a collection of the student's work in an area showing growth, self-reflection, and achievement.

Positive correlation	Relationship in which high levels of one variable correspond to high levels of another.
Positive reinforcer	Pleasurable consequence given to strengthen behavior.
Postconventional Level of Morality	Stages 5 and 6 in Kohlberg's model of moral reasoning, in which individuals make moral judgments in relation to abstract principles.
PQ4R	A study strategy that has students preview, question, read, reflect, recite and review material.
Preconventional Level of Morality	Stages 1 and 2 in Kohlberg's model of moral reasoning, in which individuals make moral judgments in their own interests.
Predictive evidence	A type of criterion-related evidence of validity that exists when scores on a test are related to scores from a measure of a trait that the test could be used to predict.
Prejudice reduction	A critical goal of multicultural education; involves development of positive relationships and tolerant attitudes among students of different backgrounds.
Premack Principle	Rule stating that enjoyable activities can be used to reinforce participation in less enjoyable activities.
Preoperational Stage	Stage at which children learn to represent things in the mind (Piaget).
Presentation punishment	An aversive stimulus following a behavior, used to decrease the chances that the behavior will occur again.

Primacy Effect	The tendency for items at the beginning of a list to be recalled more easily than other items.
Primary reinforcer	Food, water, or other consequence that satisfies a basic need.
Principle	Explanation of the relationship between factors, such as the effects of alternative grading systems on student motivation.
Private Speech	Children's self-talk, which guides their thinking and action; eventually internalized as silent inner speech (Vygotsky).
Proactive facilitation	Increased ability to learn new information due to the presence of previously acquired information.
Proactive inhibition	Decreased ability to learn new information, caused by interference from existing knowledge.
Problem solving	The application of knowledge and skills to achieve certain goals.
Problem-solving assessment	Test that calls for organizing, selecting, and applying complex procedures that have at least several important steps or components.
Problem-solving program	Program designed specifically to develop students' critical thinking skills.
Procedural memory	A part of long-term memory that stores information about how to do things.
Process-product studies	Research approach in which the teaching practices of effective teachers are recorded through classroom observation.

Prosocial behaviors	Actions that show respect and caring for others.
Psychosocial Crisis	According to Erikson, the set of critical issues that individuals must address as they pass through each of the eight life stages.
Psychosocial Theory	A set of principles that relates social environment to psychological development.
Puberty	Developmental stage at which a person becomes capable of reproduction.
Public Law 94-142	Federal law enacted in 1975 requiring provision of special education services to eligible students.
Pull-out programs	Compensatory education programs in which students are placed in separate classes for remediation.
Punishment	Unpleasant consequences used to weaken behavior.
QAIT model	A model of effective instruction that focuses on elements teachers can directly control; quality, appropriateness, incentive, and time.
Race	Visible genetic characteristics of individuals that cause them to be seen as members of the same broad group (e.g., African, Asian, Caucasian).
Random assignment	Selection by chance into different treatment groups; intended to ensure equivalence of the groups.

Randomized field experiment	Experiment conducted under realistic conditions in which individuals are assigned by chance to receive different practical treatments or programs.
Reading Recovery	A program in which specially trained teachers provide one-to-one tutoring to first graders who are not reading adequately.
Readiness tests	Tests to assess a student's levels of the skills and knowledge necessary for a given activity.
Readiness training	Instruction in the background skills and knowledge that prepare children for formal teaching later.
Recency effect	The tendency for items at the end of a list to be recalled more easily than other items.
Reciprocal teaching	A small-group teaching method based on principles of question generation; through instruction and modeling, teachers foster metacognitive skills primarily to improve the reading performance of students who have poor comprehension.
Reflectivity	The tendency to analyze oneself and one's own thoughts.
Reflexes	Inborn, automatic responses to stimuli (e.g., eye blinking in response to bright light).
Regrouping	A method of ability grouping in which students in mixed-ability classes are assigned to reading or math classes on the basis of their performance levels.

Rehearsal	Mental repetition of information, which can improve its retention.
Reinforcer	A pleasurable consequence that maintains or increases a behavior.
Relative grading standard	Grades given according to a student's rank in his or her class or grade.
Reliability	A measure of the consistency of test scores obtained from the same students at different times.
Removal punishment	Withdrawal of a pleasant consequence that is reinforcing a behavior, designed to decrease the chances that the behavior will recur.
Response to Intervention	Policies in which struggling children are given intensive assistance and are evaluated for possible special education services only if they fail to respond.
Retroactive facilitation	Increased comprehension of previously learned information due to the acquisition of new information.
Retroactive inhibition	Decreased ability to recall previously learned information, caused by learning of new information.
Reversibility	The ability to perform a mental operation and then reverse one's thinking to return to the starting point (Piaget).
Rote learning	Memorization of facts or associations that might be essentially arbitrary.

Rule-example-rule	Pattern of teaching concepts by presenting a rule or definition, giving examples, and then showing how examples illustrate the rule.
Scaffolding	Support for learning and problem solving; might include clues, reminders, encouragement, breaking the problems down into steps, providing an example, or anything else that allows the student to grow in independence as a learner (Vygotsky).
Schedule of reinforcement	The frequency and predictability of reinforcement.
Schemes	Mental patterns that guide behavior (Piaget).
Schema Theory	Theory stating that information is stored in long-term memory in schemata (networks of connected facts and concepts), which provide a structure for making sense of new information.
Schemata	Mental networks of related concepts that influence understanding of new information; the singular is *schema*.
Seatwork	Work that students are assigned to do independently during class.
Secondary reinforcer	A consequence that people learn to value through its association with a primary reinforcer.
Selected response items	Test items in which respondents can select from one or more possible answers, without requiring the scorer to interpret their response.
Self-actualization	A person's ability to develop his or her full potential (Maslow).

Self-concept	A person's perception of his or her own strengths, weaknesses, abilities, attitudes, and values.
Self-esteem	The value each of us places on our own characteristics, abilities, and behaviors.
Self-regulated learners	Students who have knowledge of effective learning strategies and how and when to use them.
Self-regulation	Rewarding or punishing one's own behavior (Bandura).
Self-regulation	The ability to think and solve problems without the help of others (Vygotsky).
Self-questioning strategies	Learning strategies that call on students to ask themselves who, what, where, and how questions as they read material.
Semantic memory	A part of long-term memory that stores facts and general knowledge.
Sensory impairments	Problems with the ability to receive information through the body's senses.
Sensory Register	Component of the memory system in which information is received and held for very short periods of time.
Sensorimotor Stage	Stage during which infants learn about their surroundings by using their senses and motor skills (Piaget).
Serial learning	Memorization of a series of items in a particular order.
Seriation	Arranging objects in sequential order according to one aspect, such as size, weight, or volume (Piaget).

Sex-role behavior

Socially approved behavior associated with one gender as opposed to the other.

Shaping

The teaching of a new skill or behavior by means of reinforcement for small steps toward the desired goal.

Short essay item

A test question the answer to which may range from a sentence or two to a page of 100 to 150 words.

Short-term or Working memory

The component of memory in which limited amounts of information can be stored for a few seconds.

Sign systems

Symbols that cultures create to help people think, communicate, and solve problems (Vygotsky).

Simulation software

Computer programs that model real-life phenomena to promote problem-solving abilities and motivate interest in the areas concerned.

Single-case experiment

Experiment that studies a treatment's effect on one person or one group by contrasting behavior before, during, and after application of the treatment.

Skinner box

An apparatus developed by B.F. Skinner for observing animal behavior in experiments in operant conditioning.

Small-group discussion

A discussion among four to six students in a group working independently of a teacher.

Small muscle development

Development of dexterity of the fine muscles of the hand.

Social comparison	The process of comparing oneself to others to gather information and to evaluate and judge one's abilities, attitudes, and conduct.
Social Learning Theory	Learning theory that emphasizes not only reinforcement but also the effects of cues on thought and of thought on action.
Socioeconomic status (SES)	A measure of prestige within a social group that is most often based on income and education.
Solitary play	Play that occurs alone.
Special Education	Programs that address the needs of students with mental, emotional, or physical disabilities.
Speech disorders	Oral articulation problems, occurring most frequently among children in the early elementary school grades
Spreadsheets	Computer programs that covert data into tables, charts, and graphs.
Standard deviation	A statistical measure of the degree of dispersion in a distribution of scores.
Standardized tests	Tests that are usually commercially prepared for nationwide use and designated to provide accurate and meaningful information on students' performance relative to that of others at their age or grade levels.
Stanine score	A type of standardized score ranging from 1-9, having a mean of 5 and a standard deviation of 2.
Stem	A question or partial statement in a test item that is completed by one of several choices.

Stimuli	Environmental conditions that activate the senses; the singular is *stimulus*.
Students at risk	Students who are subject to school failure because of their own characteristics and/or because of inadequate responses to their needs by school, family, or community.
Student Teams-Achievement Divisions (STAD)	A cooperative learning method for mixed-ability groupings involving team recognition and group responsibility for individual learning.
Success For All	A comprehensive approach to prevention and early intervention for preschool, kindergarten, and grades 1 through 8, with one-to-one tutoring, family support services, and changes in instruction designed to prevent students from falling behind.
Summarizing	Writing brief statements that represent the main idea of the information being read.
Summative assessment	Final evaluations of students' achievement of an objective.
Table of specifications	A list of instructional objectives and expected levels of understanding that guides test development.
Task analysis	Breaking tasks down into fundamental subskills.
Taxonomy of educational objectives	Bloom's ordering of objectives from simple learning tasks to more complex ones.
Teaching objectives	Clear statements of what students are intended to learn through instruction.

Teacher efficacy	The degree to which teachers feel that their own efforts determine the success of their students.
Theory	A set of principles that explains and relates certain phenomena.
Time-on-task or engaged time	Time students spend actively engaged in learning the task at hand.
Time out	Removal of a student from a situation in which misbehavior was being reinforced.
Title I	Compensatory programs reauthorized under Title I of the Improving America's Schools Act (IASA) in 1994; formerly known as Chapter 1.
Tracks	Curriculum sequences to which students of specified achievement or ability level are assigned.
Treatment	A special program that is the subject of an experiment.
Transfer of learning	The application of knowledge acquired in one situation to new situations.
Transitivity	A skill learned during the concrete operational stage of cognitive development in which individuals can mentally arrange and compare objects (Piaget).
True-false items	A form of multiple-choice test items, most useful when a comparison of two alternatives is called for.
Tutorial programs	Computer programs that teach new material, varying their content and pace according to the student's responses.

Unconditioned response	A behavior that is prompted automatically by a stimulus.
Unconditioned stimulus	A stimulus that naturally evokes a particular response.
Uncorrelated variables	Variables for which there is no relationship between high/low levels of one and high/low levels of the other.
Untracking	A focus on having students in mixed-ability groups and holding them to high standards but providing many ways for students to reach those standards.
Validity	A measure of the degree to which a test is appropriate for its intended use.
Variable	Something that can have more than one value.
Variable-Interval schedule	Reinforcement schedule in which desired behavior is rewarded following an unpredictable amount of time.
Variable-Ratio (VR) schedule	Reinforcement schedule in which desired behavior is rewarded following an unpredictable number of behaviors.
Verbal learning	Learning of words (or facts expressed in words).
Vicarious learning	Learning based on observations of the consequences of others' behavior.
Videodiscs	Interactive computer technology (might include videos, still pictures, and music).

Vision loss	Degree of uncorrectable inability to see well.
Wait time	Length of time that a teacher waits for student to answer a question.
Within-class ability grouping	A system of accommodating student differences by dividing a class of students into two or more ability groups for instruction in certain subjects.
Withitness	The degree to which the teacher is aware of and responsive to student behavior at all times.
Whole-class discussion	A discussion among all the students in the class with the teacher as moderator.
Whole language	Educational philosophy that emphasizes the integration of reading, writing, and language and communication skills across the curriculum in the context of authentic or real-life materials, problems, and tasks.
Word processing or desktop publishing	A computer application for writing compositions that lends itself to revising and editing.
Working memory	The component of memory in which limited amounts of information can be stored for a few seconds; also known as *short-term memory*.
Z-score	A standard score having a mean of 0 and a standard deviation of 1.
Zone of Proximal Development	Level of development immediately above a person's present level (Vygotsky).

SECTION 3: PRACTICE TESTS

The following practice test and the corresponding answer key is intended to give you an idea of the types of questions you can expect to encounter on the Praxis II pedagogy tests, requiring conceptual knowledge of educational psychology. You will see examples of case histories, corresponding and multiple-choice questions, constructed-response questions, and discrete multiple-choice questions. The answer key for these questions is provided below. Although mastery of these items does not guarantee passing the Praxis II pedagogy tests, they will certainly enhance your preparation to tackle the challenge to come. It is suggested that you complete these items, and then compare your responses to the answers in the key. For those items you missed, review the appropriate sections in the text to find why you were not correct. Understand that errors are inevitable, and are a necessary part of learning.

Case Histories

Case History 1

Denny Wilson is a high school Algebra Trigonometry teacher. Denny just handed back Friday's math quizzes, and is distraught over his students' performance. One young man, Juan Carlos, having failed the quiz thoroughly, crumbled his quiz, and shot it at the wastebasket, mimicking a basketball shot. Having successfully made the basket, and still holding his right arm in his follow through, Juan Carlos said: "I don't even know why we have to learn this stuff; it doesn't do us any good in life anyway. Besides, I'm going to be a pro basketball player." Denny, already feeling down about the results, shook his head in disgust at Juan Carlos's remark, and turned to Juan and said: "you see, that's why you don't do well in class, you don't treat your school work seriously. You can't go through life ignoring your obligations and expecting to do well. Besides, the chances of you making it as a pro basketball player are slim to none; you're too short. As for the rest of you," he continued, "you need to stop wasting your time fooling around and pay attention to your homework. I never failed even one quiz in math." Mr. Wilson marched back to his desk, angrily, and ordered his students to rework all the problems on the quiz, even the students who did well on the quiz. Juan, laughed out loud at Mr. Wilson's comments to maintain his classmates' esteem, but inside he felt embarrassed and hurt.

Question: Critique Denny Wilson's responses to Juan Carlos and to the class's performance on the math quiz in the context of expert teaching. How would have an expert teacher responded to these events? Write an example response to Juan Carlos's comment and to the class after the quiz.

Case History 2

Ms. Pavic's second grade class is working on reading in ability groups. To facilitate learning, Ms. Pavic invited fifth graders to help. This is a mutually beneficial arrangement because the fifth graders enjoy helping, and the second graders enjoy having their older peers help. In one grouping, the Sparrows, Rachel is helping Monica read a story about a lost puppy. Rachel doesn't read for Monica, but helps her by sounding out difficult words, and asking questions that promote thinking at higher levels than Monica is used to. Rachel also has the Sparrows discuss the reading in a free format, encouraging creative thinking.

Question: Discuss Ms. Pavic's approach in terms of Vygotsky's sociocultural theory of cognitive development. What strategies are being used by Rachel to help Monica learn to read and comprehend reading independently?

Case History 3

You have a student who is Hispanic in your class, whose name is Belén Martinez, and her parents only speak Spanish at home. In school, Belén communicates in English 100% of the time, and the parents have told you that they are concerned that their child will no longer speak Spanish to them at home -- she understands what they are saying, but only responds to them in English.

Question: Looking at Erik Erikson's and James Marcia's stages of development, what would each of them say about this student? Where would this student fall on each of their developmental stages? Briefly justify your choice.

Case History 4

It's been a hard day for Shenequa Francis. Shenequa is a teacher at George Washington high school, in her fifth year. Although Shenequa enjoys her job enormously and is highly motivated and intelligent, she has never had a challenge like the one she is faced with this year. Billy Martin is a 9th grader diagnosed with attention deficit hyperactivity disorder (ADHD). Billy was assigned to Shenequa for Algebra class, and has been a chore to handle, particularly when not taking his medication; Billy routinely walks about the class interrupting students with poor jokes. When medicated, Billy is much easier to handle. Unfortunately, it's not easy to insure that Billy takes his medication regularly. Further, Shenequa remembers learning about ADHD in college, and would like to use her learning to make the environment more conducive to all students, including those challenged with ADHD. Today was a really difficult day, as Billy spilled a soda all over a girl sitting next to him after trying to balance the soda can upon his head.

Question: What techniques are useful for teachers challenged with ADHD students that would make the classroom accessible to all students, while promoting attention to work, not distraction?

Case History 5

Margarita Jimenez, a ninth grade mathematics teacher, begins each class period with a math problem on the overhead. When the tardy bell rings, she gives students who are busy working on the problems an extra five participation points for the day. Now the majority of the students are consistently in their seats and working on the problems when the tardy bell rings.

Question: What approach is Margarita taking with her students? Do you expect the same results over time, or should Margarita alter her approach with time? Would you expect better results with negative reinforcement or punishment? Distinguish between the two and explain your response.

Case History 6

Asif is a first grader in Mr. Packing's classroom. Today, Mr. Packing is introducing students to the concept of money. He asks Asif to identify the coin that is smaller than a nickel, silver in color, but is more valuable. Asif smiles confidently, and with enthusiasm says, "A quarter!" Several girls who have had some prior experience with money giggle out loud at Asif's response. Mr. Packing wrinkles his brow, shakes his head in dismay, and quickly says, " Wow! Fran, can you tell me what coin I am looking for?" Fran says, "It's a dime!" Mr. Packing enthusiastically reinforces Fran's response with a "Great job, Fran!" – a distinctly different response than he gave Asif only a moment ago. Asif puts his head down on the desk and does not raise his hand again during the rest of this lesson.

Question: What is wrong with Mr. Packing's approach with his first graders? What approach should he take?

Case History 7

Vlade is excited to play the piano. Every day after school, he visits his piano instructor, Mr. Ivanov, and plays for an hour enthusiastically. Commenting on Vlade's enthusiasm, his parents claim that they never forced him to play the piano; "Vlade simply loves to play piano. We don't put any pressure on him; it's almost as if he'd rather play the piano than eat!" In contrast to young Vlade, Michael hates playing the piano but goes to lessons because he knows his parents will yell at him if he tells them he doesn't want to go. Michael practices daily but only to avoid a scolding at the hands of his mother and father. Michael comments: "it's like their whole life is me playing the piano. I mean I enjoy it, but I am really going to hate it if they don't let me have a little fun."

Question: Discuss motivation in the context of Vlade and Michael's experience with piano lessons. What forms of motivation are evident in the two examples? What could Michael's parents and piano instructor do, if anything, to improve Michael's experience with piano?

Case History 8

Antonio Marietta is a first year history teacher at William James junior high school. Although most of his students are very motivated, one student, Frank is causing Antonio much grief. Frank is disruptive and disrespectful of other students, constantly interrupting the class to tell jokes. Although his jokes aren't always funny, Frank is beginning to divert other students' attention from class work, and now several students are beginning to disrupt class equal to Frank. Antonio now fears he is losing control of the classroom.

Question: How could Antonio incorporate a group consequence system to reduce student misbehavior? Give an example. What benefits and pitfalls are there to group consequence systems?

Case History 9

Maia took several standardized tests at school and her scores were recently sent home to her parents. Maia obtained a standard score of 100 on one test, scored at the 50th percentile on another test, obtained a score of 75 percent on another test, and tested at the 6.4 grade equivalent level on yet another test. Unfortunately, Maia does not understand the concepts of standard scores, percentile ranks, grade equivalents, or percentages. Therefore, she is left wondering if she did well on the tests.

Question: Help Maia understand her performance by explaining the difference between standard scores, percentile ranks, percentages, and grade equivalents, and interpret her scores for her. Is there something missing that we do not know about Maia, and what should we not assume about her?

Multiple-choice and short-answer questions

1. Effective teaching is _____.
   a) research plus decision making
   b) common sense plus research
   c) reading plus common sense
   d) principles plus theory

2. "Someone who is better than average in reading is usually better than average in math," is an example of what type of correlation?
   a) permanent correlation
   b) positive correlation
   c) negative correlation
   d) no correlation at all

3. What types of research look at the strength of relationships between variables?
   a) descriptive and laboratory research
   b) single-case experiments and ethnographies
   c) correlational and experimental research
   d) static and passive research

4. Which of the following is NOT a characteristic of an effective teacher?
   a) The teacher has taught for at least five years.
   b) The teacher knows the content.
   c) The teacher understands the developmental levels and needs of the children.
   d) The teacher knows how to respond to individual differences.

5. Educational research provides evidence for all of the following EXCEPT:
   a) principles of effective practice.
   b) effective programs.
   c) choosing independent variables.
   d) selecting specific curricula.

6. Experimental research is valid only when _____
   a) it is conducted in a laboratory
   b) there is random assignment of the subjects
   c) there is a positive correlation
   d) there is no correlation

7. According to Piaget, adjusting schemes in response to the environment is called _____.
   a) reversibility
   b) equilibrium
   c) adaptation
   d) centration

8. Hypothetical reasoning occurs during which of Piaget's stages of cognitive development?
   a) presensorimotor
   b) preoperational
   c) concrete operational
   d) formal operational

9. Constructivists believe that children learn ____
   a) by seeing
   b) by hearing
   c) by doing
   d) by smelling

10. Piaget's four stages of development include all of the following except ____
    a) presensorimotor
    b) sensorimotor
    c) preoperational
    d) formal operational

11. According to Vygotsky's view of cognitive development, scaffolding means ____.
    a) a child is an independent learner
    b) a child is assisted by an adult
    c) a child watches the teacher
    d) a child demonstrates the skill for the teacher

12. The role of private speech, in Vygotsky's view, is to
    a) satisfy the egocentric needs of concrete operational children
    b) guide one's activities in solving a problem
    c) call attention to oneself during play activities
    d) stimulate the development of language from babbling to full sentences

13. Requiring students to complete their own science project is most appropriate during which stage of Erickson's stages of development?
    a) initiation versus guilt
    b) industry versus inferiority
    c) identity versus role confusion
    d) intimacy versus isolation

14. Piaget's autonomous stage of morality is similar to Kohlberg's ____ level of morality.
    a) preconventional
    b) instrumental
    c) conventional
    d) postconventional

15. Large and small muscles are characteristically developed during _____.
    a) adulthood
    b) adolescence
    c) middle childhood
    d) early childhood

16. The purpose of preschool includes all of the following EXCEPT:
    a) to develop children's social skills.
    b) to toilet-train children.
    c) to prepare children to follow directions.
    d) to improve coordination.

17. The stage where students are rapidly developing memory and cognitive skills is
    _____
    a) adulthood
    b) adolescence
    c) middle childhood
    d) early childhood

18. An example of the Vygotsky notion of scaffolding would be
    a) a teacher passing out new study materials
    b) self scoring of tests by students
    c) use of prompting during the test when a student has difficulty
    d) development of items and problems oriented to the lowest level of class readers

19. Learning in the early elementary grades is important because in our society, school success is often equated with success in _____
    a) mathematics
    b) social studies
    c) reading
    d) science

20. Advocates of developmentally appropriate practice recommend extensive use of all of the following EXCEPT
    a) projects.
    b) tests.
    c) learning centers.
    d) play.

21. Nursery schools most often serve _____ families
    a) poor
    b) middle class
    c) wealthy
    d) childless

22. The primary grades will normally be spent working through Erikson's _____ stage
    a) trust versus mistrust
    b) autonomy versus doubt
    c) initiative versus guilt
    d) industry versus inferiority

23. Erikson, in stage two of his theory of psychosocial development, asserts that parents who are overly restrictive and harsh give their children
    a) power assertion.
    b) a sense of powerlessness and incompetence, that can lead to shame and doubt in one's abilities.
    c) love withdrawal.
    d) a sense of power that can move the child towards independence.

24. The beginning of the adolescent period of development is marked by the onset of _____
    a) parental conflict
    b) peer acceptance
    c) puberty
    d) self doubt

25. Research investigates all of the following demographic student characteristics and any effects they may have on teaching and learning EXCEPT:
    a) height and weight.
    b) abilities and disabilities.
    c) race and ethnicity.
    d) gender and socioeconomic status.

26. Which student is likely to score higher on a standardized test?
    a. an impoverished student
    b. students whose homes have an abundance of books
    c. students who are required to attend summer school
    d. students whose parents attended high school only

27. Children from low-income families are placed at-risk for all of the following reasons EXCEPT
    a) the characteristics of their communities
    b) the schools they attend
    c) inadequate health services
    d) compensatory preschools

28. Research indicates that African American, Latino, and Native American students consistently score _____ their European American classmates.
    a) the same as
    b) lower than
    c) higher than
    d) just as inconsistent as

29. Research regarding effective instruction for English Language Learners suggests that language-minority students instructed in their native language as well as English perform, on average,
    a) worse on English reading measures than language-minority students instructed only in English
    b) exactly the same on English reading measures as language-minority students instructed only in English
    c) better on English reading measures than language-minority students instructed only in English
    d) no one has done any research on this question.

30. Which of the following factors is least likely to influence the amount children are likely to learn?
    a) prior knowledge
    b) intelligence
    c) motivation
    d) height

31. Mr. Lapon's classroom is the least restrictive environment for his students with special needs. What does least restrictive environment mean in this case?
    a) Mr. Lapon's classroom has the most open space for the students.
    b) Mr. Lapon's classroom is the most appropriate learning environment for each of the students with special needs.
    c) The special education classroom is full.
    d) Mr. Lapon's classroom does not have as many rules as other third-grade classrooms.

32. The students in Mr. Wilson's class whose first language is not English are in a bilingual program. What would a bilingual education program look like?
    a) The students would first learn in English and then relearn in their first language.
    b) The students would learn in English and in their first language at the same time.
    c) The students would learn in their first language and then in English.
    d) The students would learn in English only.

33. Photographs and word problems in the textbooks used in Mr. Connor's classroom depict females as nurses and males as doctors. What type of bias is portrayed?
    a) racial bias
    b) low socioeconomic bias
    c) gender bias
    d) culture bias

34. In Gardner and Thatch's eight intelligences, which of the following does NOT belong?
    a) logical/mathematical
    b) linguistic
    c) naturalist
    d) spiritual

35. Mr. Jimenez decides to offer five extra credit points for re-writing the essay on the American Revolution. The extra credit participation points serve as a _____
    a) punisher
    b) reinforcer
    c) reinforcement
    d) rehearsal

36. "Good job!" and "Way to go!" are forms of:
    a) positive reinforcement
    b) verbal warnings
    c) intrinsic reinforcers
    d) negative reinforcers

37. ___ is a consequence that strengthens behavior, while a _____ is a consequence that weakens behavior.
    a) Punishment; motivation
    b) Reinforcement; motivation
    c) Reinforcement; punishment
    d) Punishment; reinforcement

38. Getting good grades is important to Cheryl. Grades are a form of _____ reinforcement.
    a) primary
    b) secondary
    c) negative
    d) neutral

39. Felipe's sister wanted to encourage him to read more difficult books. He likes to have his sister read to him, and going to the bookstore to buy a new book is especially exciting. However, he really despises doing his math homework. His sister says, "Felipe, if you finish the ten math problems you have for homework, then I will take you to the bookstore to buy the new Harry Potter book and we can take turns reading it." This is an example of _____.
   a) the Premack Principle
   b) a removal punishment
   c) no reinforcement
   d) a neutral punisher

40. In order to prepare the students to complete their science projects, Samantha introduces them to the inquiry process by working through an experiment with the whole class. On the first day, Samantha talks with the students about hypothesizing or forming a question. Each day Samantha and her class complete an additional step in the process. Samantha is _____ the behavior of her students.
   a) persuading
   b) shaping
   c) training
   d) motivating

41. Gerry Benson's third graders are learning how to write a book report. In order to motivate them to read for the report, he gives them stickers for every five pages read. These students are on a _____ schedule of reinforcement.
   a) fixed-ratio
   b) variable ratio
   c) fixed-interval
   d) variable interval

42. Which characteristic does NOT belong: In general, students pay attention to role models who are:
   a) attractive
   b) successful
   c) interesting
   d) complex

43. Gerry's third grade students know that he expects them to clean off their whiteboards after their answers are displayed. In September, Gerry reminded them to wipe off their boards after every problem was completed. By the end of October, each student knew the routine and rarely had to be reminded to wipe their boards. These learners are best described as _____ learners.
   a) self-regulated
   b) motivated
   c) simple
   d) intelligent

44. In order to help her students remember the order of the planets, Ruby Kaster taught her students to recite the following sentence: "My very educated mother just served us nine pickles." This is an example of using ___.
    a) paired-associate learning
    b) imagery
    c) a mnemonic device
    d) serial learning

45. Sid Castillo, a fifth grade teacher at Waynesville Elementary School, was driving home when he saw an advertisement selling evergreen trees. The phone number was on the sign, but Sid could not stop to write down the number. Instead, he started repeating the number several times until he finally arrived home. Sid wrote down the phone number and called about the trees later that evening. The phone number was stored in Sid's:
    a) long-term memory.
    b) working memory.
    c) phone number memory.
    d) episodic memory.

46. Following from the last item, why did Sid rehearse the number so often?
    a) He repeated the phone number in order to transfer the phone number from his working memory to his long-term memory.
    b) He repeated the phone number frequently to transfer the phone number from his long-term memory to his short-term memory.
    c) He repeated the phone number frequently so that he could connect the number to a similar number.
    d) He repeated the phone number until he could create a simple song about the number.

47. "Knowing" how to ride a bike demonstrates what type of memory?
    a) episodic memory
    b) semantic memory
    c) procedural memory
    d) processing memory

48. One example of _____ is "learning Spanish first may help an English-speaking person later learn Italian, a similar language."
    a) proactive facilitation
    b) interference
    c) proactive inhibition
    d) retroactive facilitation

49. Margarite Jimenez coaches the freshman basketball team after school. She requires the basketball players to shoot free throws at practice. What kind of practice is exemplified in this routine?
    a) massed practice
    b) distributed practice
    c) enactment
    d) automatic

50. Memorizing the chemical symbols for the elements is a form of _____ learning.
    a) meaningful
    b) rote
    c) routine
    d) relevant

51. Which of the following is NOT a study strategy to help students learn?
    a) note-taking
    b) underlining
    c) mapping
    d) questioning

52. Enhancing long-term memory can be accomplished in all of the following ways EXCEPT through
    a) level of processing.
    b) time of day processing.
    c) dual code processing.
    d) parallel distributed processing.

53. Sean Lambert's third graders are working on multiplication in their mathematics unit. Jung continually confuses the result of three plus three and three times three. After all, two plus two is four and two times two is four. Which of the following would explain why Jung is forgetting that three times three is nine?
    a) interference
    b) retroactive inhibition
    c) proactive inhibition
    d) proactive facilitation

54. Direct instruction is more appropriate for knowing all of the following EXCEPT _____.
    a) who
    b) what
    c) when
    d) how

55. Choral response is best used when _____.
   a) there are many possible answers
   b) there is one possible answer
   c) there are two possible answers
   d) never

56. Which of the following is least true concerning independent practice time?
   a) Give clear instructions.
   b) Independent practice assignments should be at least a half hour in length.
   c) Collect independent work and include it in student grades.
   d) Monitor independent work.

57. Small group discussions are more beneficial to _____ students.
   a) second and third grade
   b) poorly organized
   c) fourth and fifth grade
   d) all of the above

58. Which of the following is NOT a part of a direct instruction lesson?
   a) State learning objectives and orient students to the lesson.
   b) Present new material.
   c) Assess performance and provide feedback.
   d) Group reflections and presentations.

59. Which of the following is the best example of a learning probe?
   a) a unit test
   b) a homework assignment
   c) in-class practice
   d) a standardized test

60. The teacher's role is least dominant in which lesson type?
   a) whole-class discussions
   b) lectures
   c) small-group discussions
   d) individualized instruction

61. A constructivist approach to teaching is best described as
   a) a top-down approach, complex problems to basic problems.
   b) a bottom-up approach, basic problems to more complex problems.
   c) a variable approach, sometimes complex to basic problems and other times basic to complex problems.
   d) a mixture of complex and basic problems.

62. Which of the following exemplifies critical thinking?
    a) identifying the sum of two numbers
    b) identifying the dates of the Civil War
    c) identifying assumptions in an argument
    d) identifying middle C on a piano

63. Problem-solving strategies should consider all of the following, EXCEPT
    a) What resources and information are available?
    b) How can the problem be represented?
    c) What problem needs to be solved?
    d) How can the problem be duplicated?

64. Teaching children to work cooperatively does NOT include teaching which of the following skills?
    a) active listening
    b) including most members of the group
    c) avoiding putdowns
    d) giving good examples

65. To ensure student learning, John Carroll described teaching in terms of all of the following EXCEPT
    a) management of time.
    b) management of skills.
    c) management of resources.
    d) management of activities.

66. The amount of class time that is actually available for learning largely depends on the amount of time that the teacher schedules for _____ and the amount of time _____
    a) instruction; actually used to teach
    b) recess; actually used to teach
    c) reading; scheduled for math
    d) morning meetings; actually used to teach

67. Ability-grouping is commonly used in which subjects?
    a) mathematics and science
    b) science and reading
    c) mathematics and reading
    d) reading and social studies

68. Students in _____ are far more likely than other students to become delinquent.
    a) the high-track
    b) the average-track
    c) the low-track
    d) a mixed-ability group

69. One of the most effective instructional strategies that essentially solves the problem of appropriate levels of instruction is
    a) one-to-one adult-to-child tutoring
    b) one-to-one child-to-child tutoring
    c) peer tutoring to a small group of students
    d) same-age peer tutoring

70. All of the following are uses for computer-based instruction EXCEPT
    a) as a tutor to present information.
    b) to give students practice.
    c) to assess level of understanding.
    d) to word process short stories.

71. Which of the following is NOT a characteristic of students placed at-risk?
    a) They are from single parent home households
    b) They are marked with development delays
    c) Their parent(s) work outside of the home
    d) They exhibit aggressive or withdrawn behavior

72. Title I money can only be used to _____
    a) reduce class size for all students.
    b) supplement local funds to increase the academic achievement of disadvantaged students.
    c) increase teacher salaries in schools with disadvantaged students.
    d) replace local funds to increase the academic achievement of disadvantaged students.

73. Tutors should do all of the following EXCEPT
    a) use corrective feedback.
    b) alternate teaching methods/materials.
    c) do the work for the tutee.
    d) prompt responses from tutee.

74. Computer-assisted instruction (CAI) programs usually share what characteristic?
    a) They use a flexible curriculum
    b) They make students work at the same pace
    c) They measure performance once the program is completed
    d) They give students reinforcement

75. Maslow's deficiency needs are those needs that must be satisfied. These needs include all of the following EXCEPT
    a) self-esteem needs.
    b) physiological needs.
    c) belongingness and love needs.
    d) aesthetic needs.

76. The attribution theory for explaining success and failure deals with all of the following EXCEPT
    a) ability.
    b) task difficulty.
    c) motivation.
    d) luck.

77. _____ is the most important predictor of a student's success.
    a) Ability
    b) Task difficulty
    c) Motivation
    d) Luck

78. If you, as a teacher, wanted to use ongoing, frequent assessments of student learning in order to adjust your instruction to meet the individual needs of your students, the best method would probably be to use
    a) final examinations
    b) formative assessment
    c) SAT's
    d) summative assessment

79. Which of the following is NOT a way that teachers can communicate positive expectation for their students?
    a) use short wait times for students to respond
    b) avoid unnecessary achievement distinctions among students
    c) treat all students equally
    d) move students in and out of groups when appropriate

80. What can be said about a student's intrinsic motivation throughout the school years?
    a) Intrinsic motivation generally increases from elementary school to secondary school.
    b) Intrinsic motivation is the same in elementary school as in high school.
    c) Intrinsic motivation generally decreases from elementary school to secondary school.
    d) Most students are not intrinsically motivated at all.

81. Which of the following is NOT true for motivating students to learn?
    a) Express clear expectations.
    b) Provide clear feedback.
    c) Provide the same motivators at all times.
    d) Provide immediate feedback.

82. Which of the following is LEAST true concerning motivation?
    a) Motivation levels rarely change.
    b) Motivation is difficult to measure.
    c) Motivation is a critical component of learning.
    d) All students are motivated.

83. A person with an internal locus of control is more likely to believe that _____ cause(s) success or failure.
    a) luck
    b) his or her own efforts
    c) task difficulty
    d) other people's actions

84. Effective learning environments _____.
    a) prevent misbehavior
    b) provide stimulating lessons
    c) challenge students
    d) do all of the above

85. The number of minutes actually spent learning is called _____
    a) class time
    b) time on-task
    c) measured time
    d) time allocated

86. Which of the following is true about classroom rules?
    a) Classroom rules should be established at the beginning of the year.
    b) Students should create all of the rules.
    c) There should be a rule for every infraction.
    d) Classroom procedures should be flexible.

87. Which of the following is least effective for handling minor misbehavior?
    a) Using nonverbal cues.
    b) Praising behavior that is incompatible with misbehavior.
    c) Avoiding the use of consequences.
    d) Praising other students.

88. One effective punishment for a student who continually acts out in class is
    a) to call the student's name and give a verbal reminder.
    b) to give the student a time-out in another classroom.
    c) to ignore the student's actions.
    d) to use physical punishment.

89. "We will go to lunch when everyone has put away their library books," is an example of
    a) a group contingency program.
    b) an individualized program.
    c) a home-based reinforcement program.
    d) a point accumulation program.

90. Why do students misbehave?
    a) To get the teacher's attention.
    b) To get released from an undesirable activity.
    c) To get the attention of their peers.
    d) All of the above.

91. _____ is a systematic application of antecedents and consequences to change behavior.
    a) Punishment
    b) Extinction
    c) Behavior modification
    d) Group contingency program

92. _____ is/are the easiest approach to dealing with behavioral problems.
    a) Preventive programs
    b) Enforcing rules and practices
    c) Enforcing school attendance
    d) Avoiding tracking

93. Students who are identified by an IQ test as being gifted and/or talented usually score _____ standard deviations above the mean of 100.
    a) one
    b) two
    c) three
    d) four

94. Who is eligible for special education services?
    a) students with physical disabilities
    b) students with mental disabilities
    c) students with behavioral disabilities
    d) all of the above

95. Cognitive impairment, as described by the American Association on Mental Retardation (AAMR), is determined by all of the following EXCEPT
    a) a student's school performance.
    b) a student's job performance.
    c) a student's IQ score.
    d) a student's cultural background.

96. Which group of students is usually NOT overrepresented in special education classes?
    a) boys
    b) African Americans
    c) Latinos
    d) girls

97. Which of the following is NOT a characteristic of student's with learning disabilities?
    a) lower academic self-esteem
    b) non-academic self-esteem similar to that of peers
    c) social dimension higher than that of other low achievers
    d) social dimension similar to that of other low achievers

98. Which of the following is a good strategy for teaching students with learning disabilities?
    a) lecture students
    b) coordinate supplemental services with classroom instruction
    c) provide monthly feedback
    d) provide a slow-paced lesson

99. All of the following are true about developing an Individualized Education Plan (IEP) EXCEPT
    a) parents must be notified.
    b) parents must give consent.
    c) students may be an active member of their IEP team.
    d) parents may not have input considered.

100.   Discuss strategies that a teacher could use when teaching students with learning disabilities.

101.   What are signs that a child has a possible visual disability that a teacher may observe?

102.   Instructional objectives, also called behavioral objectives, should have three parts. Identify which of the following is NOT part of an instructional objective.
    a) performance
    b) criterion
    c) method
    d) condition

103.   Of the following, identify the best choice for the performance verb used in an instructional objective.
    a) to know
    b) to appreciate
    c) to identify
    d) to grasp

104. _____ is the last step in backwards planning.
    a) Planning daily lessons
    b) Writing broad objectives for the whole course
    c) Writing objectives for large units
    d) Identifying units of study

105. In Bloom's taxonomy of educational objectives, _____ is the highest level of thinking.
    a) analysis
    b) application
    c) comprehension
    d) evaluation

106. Which of the following is NOT one of the principle reasons for writing instructional objectives?
    a) to improve student achievement
    b) to contrast goals and methods
    c) to guide evaluation
    d) to organize teacher planning

107. Which of the following is NOT a primary reason for student evaluations?
    a) feedback for students and teachers
    b) information for selection and certification
    c) information for policy makers
    d) incentives to increase student effort

108. Which of the following is NOT a form of a selected-response test item?
    a) multiple choice
    b) essay
    c) true-false
    d) matching items

109. All of the following are forms of performance assessment EXCEPT
    a) portfolios.
    b) dance recitals.
    c) a written driver's license test.
    d) a speech.

110. In planning a course, it is important for the teacher to set _____ objectives before starting to teach.
    a) long-term
    b) middle-term
    c) short-term
    d) all

111.   At what cognitive level is the objective, "The student will be able to identify the main idea of a story."
   a) knowledge
   b) application
   c) analysis
   d) evaluation

112.   Which test item applies concepts at the highest level of instructional objectives?
   a) true-false
   b) short essay
   c) completion
   d) matching

113.   Discuss the advantages and disadvantages of standardized testing and alternative assessments.

114.   Standardized tests are used _____.
   a) because there is little criticism about their use
   b) locally only
   c) to compare individuals or groups of students
   d) because they are inexpensive

115.   All of the following are important functions of standardized testing EXCEPT
   a) performance.
   b) diagnosis.
   c) evaluation.
   d) selection and placement.

116.   Each of the following is a form of standardized test commonly used in schools EXCEPT
   a) aptitude test.
   b) unit test.
   c) criterion-referenced test.
   d) norm-referenced test.

117.   _____ are most meaningful when they are constructed around a well-defined set of objectives. The results can be used to guide future instruction or remedial activities.
   a) Unit tests
   b) Criterion-referenced tests
   c) Norm-referenced tests
   d) Aptitude tests

118.   The _____ relates to the accuracy with which skills and knowledge are measured.
   a) content-evidence
   b) method
   c) reliability
   d) criterion-related evidence

119.   Which of the following is true about the relationship between validity and reliability?
   a) A test can be valid without being reliable.
   b) A test can be reliable without being valid.
   c) Most tests are neither valid nor reliable.
   d) Validity and reliability are distinct and there is no relationship.

120.   _____ grades provide information about what a student knows or what a student can do.
   a) Performance
   b) Traditional
   c) Standardized
   d) Unit test

121.   Of the following, which is NOT a grading approach associated with innovative instructional approaches?
   a) mastery grading
   b) contract grading
   c) performance grading
   d) criterion grading

122.   Report card grades are derived from _____
   a) quiz and test scores
   b) homework scores
   c) participation and effort scores
   d) all of the above

123.   Relative grading standards create a _____ classroom atmosphere.
   a) cooperative
   b) competitive
   c) challenging
   d) critical

124.   Which of the following is NOT a criticism of standardized testing?
   a) Standardized tests give false information about the status of learning in the nation's schools.
   b) Standardized tests are unfair (or biased) against some kinds of students (e.g., minority students, those with limited proficiency in English, females, and students from low-income families).
   c) Standardized tests tend to corrupt the processes of teaching and learning, often reducing teaching to mere preparation for testing.
   d) Standardized tests focus time, energy, and attention on the more complex, higher-order skills and creative endeavors.

125.   What are the main differences between standardized and nonstandardized tests?

ANSWER KEY TO PRACTICE TESTS

Answers to Case Histories

Case History 1, Possible answer: It is understandable that Mr. Wilson is frustrated. However, he did not handle the situation correctly either in reference to Juan Carlos's comment or the class's performance. First, he should not have scolded Juan Carlos publicly, embarrassing Juan in front of his peers, especially given Juan's developmental age, as adolescents are already highly image conscious. Second, he should not have punished all the students for the poor performance of some students. Instead, if Denny were an expert teacher, he would have used Juan Carlos's comment as an opportunity to teach the importance of mathematics in daily life. For example, he could have commented as follows: "You are right Juan, it's not always clear how math relates to daily life. However, it does; let me show you. Did you know that math is involved in sports like basketball? In fact, the stats, or statistics, you hear about basketball players, like free-throw percentage, are derived by mathematics. Let's take your basket, for example. Since you sunk your quiz, and you attempted only one shot, we have a ratio of one basket to one shot. What's one divided by one? Juan Carlos would likely respond, "It's one, of course." Right," responds Denny, "it's one." Now if you multiply it by 100, what do you get?" "You get 100," responded another classmate enthusiastically. "And then if you add a percent sign to it," writing the percent on the blackboard, you get 100%. Mr. Wilson proceeds to have the students work a number of such examples.
With respect to the overall class performance, an expert teacher could ask students to rework the problems, individually, and perhaps have classmates already understanding how to complete the math problems, help their peers. In this way, all students would be engaged in activity, social skills would be enhanced, and student understanding would improve, both for those teaching and those learning. (See Chapter 13: Assessing Student Learning)

Case History 2, Possible Answer: Ms. Pavic is attempting to facilitate cognitive development, promoting higher levels of development within her students' range of potential, what Vygotsky called "Zone of Proximal Development." To achieve this, Ms. Pavic invited older students, who possess valuable cultural knowledge, to scaffold (erecting a framework for development). Rachel is scaffolding by sounding out but not completing difficult words, and asking question that promote critical thinking. Further, Rachel's engagement of students in free discussion is an example of reciprocal teaching. Reciprocal teaching is a strategy following from Vygotsky's theory that encourages students at different levels of cognitive development to push each other to greater heights. Therefore, Ms. Pavic uses older students to promote greater cognitive achievement by having fifth graders challenge her second graders' thinking. (See Chapter 2: Theories of Development)

Case History 3, Possible Answer: Belén may be starting to think of herself as an American child, and as such sees that most of her friends speak English all the time. In order to feel like she fits in with and is more strongly influenced by her peers, she might feel that she needs to reject her native language of Spanish in favor of the language of her friends, English, rather than see herself as bilingual. Belén's parents may feel rejected or confused by her behavior, which might not fit with their own conception or experience of raising children to be bilingual. While they may support their child learning and communicating in English outside of the home, they also expect their daughter to use the primary home language, Spanish, as a means of communication in the home. According to Erik Erikson, this would place Belén in Erikson's *Identity vs. Role Confusion* stage of psychosocial development, a stage that encompasses the school years just prior to and into adolescence. Adolescents increasingly turn away from parents and toward peer groups. Erikson felt that adolescents go through a phase where they may ask themselves, "Who am I?" According to James Marcia, Belén is probably in a state of *Moratorium*, whereby she is experimenting with ideological choices, may be in the midst of an identity crisis, cannot make ideological commitments, and may be examining alternate life choices. Belén's teachers could encourage her parents to continue to speak Spanish to her at home, and at school her teachers could create opportunities for Belén to see successful bilingual role models. Presumably, she will enter Erikson's next stage of *Intimacy vs. Isolation* and Marcia's final state of *Identity Achievement*. (See Chapter 2: Theories of Development and Chapter 3: Development During Childhood and Adolescence)

Case History 4, Possible Answer: Shenequa's approach is correct. Several techniques can help her achieve her goal of making her classroom accessible to all students. First, she should carefully structure the classroom environment, by seating students with ADHD away from distractions, and near students considered "good workers." This approach will provide modeling for students like Billy. Second, activities should be well structured, providing rule clarity and *escapes* for students with difficulty concentrating for long periods of time. Third, teachers should help students focus attention, by providing mutually acceptable non-verbal attention cues, such as a tap on the shoulder. Fourth, teachers must learn to give feedback about the appropriateness of behaviors. This feedback should focus on behaviors considered good as well as those considered inappropriate, and should target all students. Finally, teachers should provide opportunities to expend excess energy, like physical activity breaks during class. For instance, Shenequa could have students engage in stretching periodically, or other light calisthenics. (See Chapter 12: Learners with Exceptionalities)

Case History 5, Possible Answer: Margarita is using a token reinforcement system with her students. This system works by reinforcing specific behaviors publicly (in the present case), and making the respondent aware of what *operant* results in reinforcement (reward). Over time, the results depend on the *schedule of reinforcement*. Initially, it is essential to reward every occurrence of the desired behavior. However, as time passes, a *partial reinforcement schedule* is preferable. *Partial reinforcement schedules* reward behavior on some proportion of total responses, differing on two key dimensions: time (interval schedule) or number (ratio schedule) of correct responses necessary to achieve reward. Interval and ratio schedules can also be fixed or variable in nature. Thus, Margarita should reward all responses initially, then reward on some partial schedule, like a *variable interval schedule* that keeps her students guessing when the next token will be distributed. Regarding negative reinforcement or punishment, better results would be expected for negative reinforcement than punishment, since punishment adds something negative (e.g., pain), whereas negative reinforcement removes something negative (e.g., a chore). Punishment is not generally as effective as reinforcement, and is wrought with problems, including encouraging further mischievous behavior. (See Chapter 5: Behavioral Theories of Learning)

Case History 6, Possible Answer: Mr. Packing's enthusiastic reinforcement of Fran's response might indicate that this teacher may not understand that children in the first grade may have different experiences with money, and therefore different levels of understanding of the concept of money. Some children are not allowed to handle money because parents fear children may swallow coins. In addition, some children are not exposed to money at this early an age because their parents have little money available; as opposed to children whose parents may buy play money and directly teach their children. Therefore, Mr. Packing should think about talking to the parents first, and encourage them to introduce the concept of money to their children, as the concept will be covered in class. If parents are unable to provide the practice for children, he could make kits of play coins that parents could borrow with activities. Mr. Packing's approach is not necessarily bad, although he should be remember that for many young children, taking a risk to respond to a question is difficult, and all responses should be courteously addressed. If he is assessing his students' prior experience with money, and will use this information to tailor his lesson plan to his class, he could have started by asking children to identify coins, their value, and relationship to one another to see what they know already. One suggestion is for Mr. Packing to avoid praising correct answers excessively and provide feedback for both correct and incorrect answers. However, before this approach, he should review his educational psychology text about concept formation. (See Chapter 7: The Effective Lesson)

Case History 7, Possible Answer: Clearly Michael and Vlade have different motives for playing piano. Because Michael plays piano to avoid his parents' reprimands, he is motivated to avoid the pain of punishment, an external force. Therefore, Michael is extrinsically motivated to play the piano. By contrast, Vlade seems to play the piano just for the sake of playing the piano; no extrinsic motive is necessary to induce him to play. Therefore, it can be concluded that Vlade is motivated intrinsically to play piano. Regarding the second part of the question, to increase Michael' intrinsic motivation, Michael's parents and his teacher must not allow Michael to feel that he is being pressured to play the piano. They can begin by giving him other opportunities to spend his free time, like letting him go to movies with his friends. Further, during piano lessons, Mr. Ivanov can give Michael greater freedom to choose what to play. To increase intrinsic motivation, one must not feel that reward is too strictly conditional on specific outcomes. Michael must feel that he is a worthwhile individual regardless of whether or not he plays piano well. (See Chapter 10: Motivating Students to Learn)

Case History 8, Possible Answer: It is never popular to punish all students for one student's transgressions. However, the unpopularity of this approach is precisely why it can be effective. Because junior high school students value social activities so much, Antonio can take away a highly valued activity for all students, a form of negative punishment, if Frank continues to disregard classroom decorum. For example, every semester Antonio likes to take his students on a field trip to visit a local historic site. He arranges for a picnic lunch where students discuss history and attend to their social needs. Antonio has been discussing the trip all semester, and students have been very receptive. By making the trip contingent on each student's behavior, it is likely that other students will police Frank's behavior because their own interests are at stake. Therefore, a strength of this approach is that other students help reinforce class decorum. Further, it is possible that knowledge of his potential to ruin everyone's fun will force Frank's behavior toward the norm. The weakness of this approach is that it could backfire if Frank doesn't care about his peers' feelings, and even enjoys holding them "hostage." Further, students could retaliate in some way against Frank for misbehaving in class. (See Chapter 11: Effective Learning Environments)

Case History 9, Possible Answer: Maia's tests were recorded as a standard score, a percentile rank, a percentage, and a grade equivalent. Standard Scores are raw scores that have been converted to reflect a particular mean and standard deviation. Standard scores demonstrate how far an individual's score is positioned from the mean in terms of the standard deviation, and on many tests (such as cognitive tests) the mean is 100. Maia's standard score of 100 would reflect an average score. Percentile ranks or norms are derived scores used to determine a student's position in relation to the standardization sample. A percentile is the score in a distribution below which a given percentage of individuals fall (e.g., if 54 percent of the sample falls below a particular score, that score is at the 54th percentile). An individual who has obtained a percentile rank of 25 scored as well or better than 25 percent of the people in the normed sample. The median score is at the 50th percentile; thus, Maia's percentile score is an average score. Percentages are not the same as percentiles, and are frequently used in a variety of assessment instruments, including teacher-made tests and criterion-referenced tests. Usually a percentage is derived based on the number of possible correct responses and can be calculated by multiplying 100 times the ratio of the number of correct responses to the number of possible responses. For example, if Maia gets 112 correct responses on a test with 150 items, her score would be 75 percent correct. Some tests, especially reading tests, indicate several levels, with corresponding percentages, intended to facilitate instruction: mastery (generally 90 percent correct) and nonmastery (generally less than 90 percent correct); and independent (generally above 95 percent correct), instructional (generally between 85 to 95 percent correct), and frustrational (generally less than 85 percent correct). A grade equivalent (GE) is usually used on tests of educational achievement, and it is found by computing the mean raw score obtained by children in each grade. For example, if the average number of problems correctly solved on a math test by third graders in the standardization sample is 23, then the raw score of 23 directly corresponds to a grade equivalent of 3. Months are expressed in decimals from 0-9, corresponding to the number of months in a school year (e.g., Maia's GE of 6.4 is equivalent to the fourth month of sixth grade or January of sixth grade). Caution should be used when interpreting grade norms: they may be most applicable for common subjects taught throughout grade levels covered by tests; scores may not represent equal units (e.g., difference between second and third grade-equivalent scores may not be the same as the difference between eleventh and twelfth grade-equivalent scores); scores may not be those actually obtained by the child; interpreting fifth grade arithmetic scores to mean that a third grade child can perform fifth grade math may be erroneous. All we know about Maia are her scores, some of which indicate average performance. What we do not know about Maia is: what grade she is currently in, how old she is, and what kinds of assessments she took (reading, cognitive, math, etc.). Therefore, caution should be exercised in making the assumption that she is an average 6th grade student.

(See Chapter 13: Assessing Student Learning and Chapter 14: Standardized Tests and Accountability)

Answers to multiple-choice and short-answer items

1. c	23. b
2. b	24. c
3. c	25. a
4. a	26. b
5. c	27. d
6. b	28. b
7. c	29. c
8. d	30. d
9. c	31. b
10. a	32. c
11. b	33. c
12. b	34. d
13. b	35. b
14. c	36. a
15. d	37. c
16. b	38. b
17. c	39. a
18. c	40. b
19. c	41. a
20. b	42. d
21. b	43. a
22. d	44. c

45. b	68. c
46. a	69. a
47. c	70. d
48. a	71. c
49. c	72. b
50. b	73. c
51. d	74. d
52. c	75. d
53. b	76. c
54. d	77. a
55. b	78. b
56. b	79. a
57. c	80. c
58. d	81. c
59. c	82. a
60. c	83. b
61. a	84. d
62. c	85. b
63. d	86. a
64. b	87. c
65. b	88. b
66. a	89. a
67. c	90. d

91. c

92. a

93. b

94. d

95. b

96. d

97. c

98. b

99. d

100. Possible Answer: The teacher should start by adapting the instruction, the content, and/or the communication mode.

101. Possible Answer: Rubbing the eyes, squinting, and watery, crusty eyes are signs that a teacher may observe in a student who is having vision problems.

102. c

103. c

104. a

105. d

106. b

107. c

108. b

109. c

110. d

111. c

112. b

113. Possible Answer: Alternative assessments like portfolios and performance assessments avoid the negative aspects of standardized tests by requiring students to demonstrate their learning. However, alternative assessments are subjective and more time consuming.

114. c

115. a

116. b

117. b

118. c

119. b

120. a

121. d

122. d

123. b

124. d

125. Possible Answer: Standardized tests provide information about what a student knows in a quick, objective, and cost-effective format. Nonstandardized tests are usually more subjective and, as a result, more expensive to use.

NOTES

NOTES

NOTES

NOTES

NOTES

NOTES

NOTES

NOTES

NOTES

NOTES

NOTES

NOTES

NOTES

NOTES

NOTES

NOTES

NOTES

NOTES

NOTES